Layer Cake,
Jelly Roll and Charm Quilts

Layer Cake,
Jelly Roll and Charm Quilts

PAM & NICKY LINTOTT

D&C

David and Charles

www.mycraftivity.com

A DAVID & CHARLES BOOK
Copyright © David & Charles Limited 2009, 2010

David & Charles is an F+W Media Inc. company
4700 East Galbraith Road
Cincinnati, OH 45236

First published in the UK and USA in 2009
Reprinted 2009 (twice), 2010

Text and designs copyright © Pam and Nicky Lintott 2009, 2010

Pam and Nicky Lintott have asserted their right to be identified as authors of
this work in accordance with the Copyright, Designs and Patents Act, 1988.

A catalogue record for this book is available from the British Library.

ISBN-13: 978-0-7153-3208-5 paperback
ISBN-10: 0-7153-3208-2 paperback

Printed in USA by RR Donnelley & Sons, Inc
for David & Charles
Brunel House, Newton Abbot, Devon

Commissioning Editor: Jane Trollope
Desk Editor: Emily Rae
Project Editor: Lin Clements
Art Editor: Sarah Clark
Production Controller: Beverley Richardson and Alison Smith
Illustrator: Ethan Danielson
Photographer: Kim Sayer and Karl Adamson

Visit our website at www.davidandcharles.co.uk

David & Charles books are available from all good bookshops; alternatively
you can contact our Orderline on 0870 9908222 or write to us at
FREEPOST EX2 110, D&C Direct, Newton Abbot, TQ12 4ZZ (no stamp
required UK only); US customers call 800-289-0963 and Canadian
customers call 800-840-5220.

Contents

Introduction

We know how much you love jelly rolls. The success of our book *Jelly Roll Quilts* really excited us and we were so encouraged by your enthusiasm. Now we have something else to be excited about – layer cakes and charm packs!

Having squares of fabric as opposed to strips opens up many more design opportunities. Never let anyone tell you that squares are boring – you could simply sew squares together and if you use coordinated and inspiring fabric it would create an easy and visually stunning quilt. Our quilts made from charm squares are still basically squares with just a few additions and changes and this creates the patchwork design. We haven't even touched on cutting up the 5in squares – that could fill another book!

The 10in squares in our layer cakes gave us scope for lots of new designs, some showing quick and easy patterns cut easily from the layer cake as in Diamonds at Large on page 24 and others such as Little Houses on page 102, which became far more intricate.

Using pre-cut fabric has many benefits: it's quick and easy and having the fabrics already coordinated means that you can get straight on with a project knowing that the colours in your finished quilt are going to blend well together. Often you will be using fabrics that you wouldn't normally choose (or be brave enough to use!) and we can assure you that often it is those fabrics that add extra sparkle to a quilt.

Our Strip Club, which we hold on the first Monday of the month at The Quilt Room, has been renamed Mystery Monday as no one knows quite what we will be using – layer cakes, jelly rolls or charm squares. Some of the quilts in this book have been introduced at our Mystery Monday mornings and some are brand new. We hope they inspire you.

Getting Started

What is a Jelly Roll?

A jelly roll is a roll of forty fabrics cut in 2½in wide strips across the width of the fabric. Moda introduced jelly rolls to showcase new fabric ranges. How inspirational to have one 2½in wide strip of each new fabric wrapped up so deliciously!

If you want to make any of the jelly roll quilts in this book and don't have a jelly roll to use, then cut a 2½in wide strip from forty fabrics in your stash and you can follow all of the instructions in just the same way.

What is a Layer Cake?

A layer cake is a stack of forty fabrics 10in square and is another brilliant way of presenting fabrics from Moda. A layer cake contains the same amount of fabric as a jelly roll (10in x 10in = 2½in x 40in) but having the fabric in a square, rather than a strip, opens up some exciting design opportunities that couldn't be achieved with strips alone.

If you want to make any of the layer cake quilts in this book and don't have a layer cake to use, just cut a 10in square from forty fabrics in your stash and you can follow all of the instructions in just the same way.

What is a Charm Pack?

Charm quilts historically are quilts in which a fabric was only used once, however small a piece it was. Therefore, only small pieces of each fabric were needed and today charm packs are very useful when 'large amounts of small amounts' are required. Charm packs do come in different sizes but for the purposes of this book we have used the 5in charm squares that Moda produce and which are proving the most popular size.

Most charm packs contain between forty and fifty squares of fabric. We have assumed that you get forty squares in a charm pack so, if you do have more, then that is a real bonus! This also means that some of the patterns for charm packs in this book are interchangeable with layer cakes. For example, if the pattern calls for four charm packs, you know that you can cut one layer cake into four charm packs and you will have the required amount of 5in squares.

Important Information

Imperial or Metric?

Jelly rolls from Moda are cut 2½in wide and at The Quilt Room we have continued to cut our strip bundles 2½in wide. Layer cakes are cut 10in square.

When quilt making, it is impossible to mix metric and imperial measurements. It would be absurd to have a 2½in strip and tell you to cut it 6cm to make a square! It wouldn't be square and nothing would fit.

This caused a dilemma when writing instructions for our quilts and a decision had to be made. All our instructions therefore are written in inches. Fabric requirements are, however, given in both imperial and metric. To convert inches to centimetres, multiply the inch measurement by 2.54.

Washing Notes

Do NOT wash that pre-cut fabric before use. Save the washing until your quilt is complete and then use a colour catcher in the wash or dry clean the quilt.

Seam Allowance

We cannot stress enough the importance of using an accurate scant ¼in seam allowance throughout. Carefully check your seam allowance with the test on page 122.

Quilt Size

In this book we have shown what can be achieved by using just one jelly roll, just one layer cake or just a few charm packs. We have sometimes used additional background fabric and borders but the basis of each quilt is just one pre-cut fabric bundle. We have also popped in a couple of patterns using just one layer cake with just one jelly roll – you may consider that this is cheating a little bit but they really do make lovely large quilts!

Diagrams

The quilt instructions have many useful diagrams to accompany them and where possible these are placed beneath the relevant instructions. Arrows on diagrams indicate the direction in which a seam should be pressed. Read all the instructions through very carefully before starting a quilt.

Charming Flowers

Vital statistics

Quilt size:	66in x 84in
Block size:	4½in
Number of blocks:	192
Setting:	12 blocks x 16 blocks plus 6in border

The following two quilts are made by sewing charm squares together and there can't be anything much easier than that. They both have some half-square triangles strategically placed and suddenly the quilts come alive. Not a lot of effort for a great reward!

This Charming Flowers quilt uses Lecien's gorgeous Japanese florals. We have introduced some darker reds as additional fat quarters to make our flowers stand out.

The only thing that you have to remember when combining charm squares with squares made up of two triangles is that they have to be the same *finished* size.

This sounds obvious but you need to know that if your finished charm squares are 4½in (which they will be if you are using 5in charm packs or dividing a layer cake), your triangles forming the half-square triangle need to be cut from a square measuring 5⅜in. Don't be put off by this as it is no more difficult to cut a square 5⅜in than it is to cut a 5in square. If you cut accurately right from the start you will have no need to trim at a later stage – so saving yourself time and effort.

If your charm squares vary from 5in – no problem. When cutting your squares from the fat quarters to make your half-square triangle units, just alter the size of the squares, remembering to add ⅞in to the finished size of your charm pack squares. Therefore if your charm squares are only 4½in (finished size 4in), you will cut 4⅞in squares for your half-square triangles.

What you need

- One layer cake **or** four charm packs
- Four fat quarters (two light and two dark) for stars
- 2¼yd (2m) fabric for borders and binding

opposite:
Squares are definitely not boring and with a few strategically placed half-square triangles a quick and easy quilt can look absolutely stunning. We chose a lovely floral quilting design to enhance the fabrics. The quilt was pieced by the authors and longarm quilted by The Quilt Room.

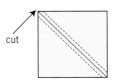

Cutting Instructions

Layer cake:

If you are using a layer cake, rotary cut the 10in square in half in both directions to create four 5in squares, as shown below. You will get 160 squares – eight will be spare and can be used for another project. If you are using charm packs, then you already have your 5in squares cut.

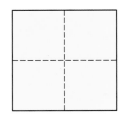

Border and binding:

- Cut four strips lengthways 6½in wide.
- Cut four strips lengthways 2½in wide. When using large florals in a border, it's preferable not to have any joins.

Seam allowance:

- Use scant ¼in seams throughout.

Making the Half-square Triangle Units

1. Layer a dark and light fat quarter with right sides together, as shown below, with the light fabric on the top, lining up the top and left-hand side.

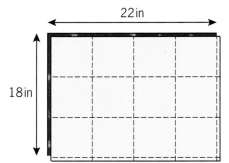

2. Press to keep the two layers together. Don't be over zealous when trimming any selvedge as you need 21½in across to be able to cut four strips.

3. Cut four strips 5⅜in wide. Sub-cut each strip into three squares each 5⅜in x 5⅜in. You need ten squares from each fat quarter – two are spare.

4. Keeping the two layers of each square together, mark a line across the diagonal of the light fabric.

5. Stitch either side of this marked line with a scant ¼in seam allowance.

6. Press to set the stitches and then cut along the marked line.

7. Trim dog ears and open, pressing towards the dark fabric. You will get twenty units.

8. Repeat with the other two fat quarters to create another twenty units. You need forty in total.

Assembling your Quilt

- Lay out all your charm squares in sixteen rows of twelve, referring to the diagram, right to see where to place your half-square triangle units.
- Some of the stars were made up using just one dark fabric and some were made up by alternating both the dark fabrics. When happy with the layout, label the first square of each row with the row number, to ensure they stay in the correct order after sewing.
- Sew the squares into rows and then join the rows together, pinning at every intersection to ensure that there is a perfect match. Press the work.

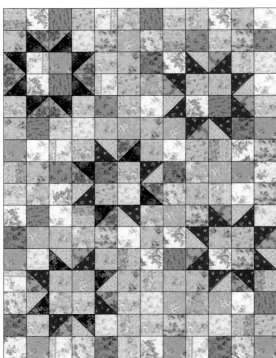

Sewing your Borders

- Refer to page 123 for adding your borders.
- Your quilt top is now complete. Quilt as desired and bind to finish (see page 124).

Times Square

Instead of making a variation of Charming Flowers, we made a different quilt that uses the same technique. Again it is squares sewn together with clever placement of half-square triangle units to create the artistic design.

We have used two charm packs from Moda's range Charisma by Chez Moi, which gives a lovely colourwash effect, together with two neutral charm packs. You could of course use one layer cake cut into 5in squares as long as there were sufficient lights to create the design.

Vital statistics

Quilt size:	63in x 63in
Block size:	4½in
Number of blocks:	196
Setting:	14 x 14 blocks

What you need

- Four charm packs – two lights and two darks (you need seventy-two of each for this quilt and will have eight of each spare for another project)
- Six fat quarters (three light and three dark) for half-square triangles
- 20in (50cm) for binding

Cutting Instructions

Binding fabric:
- Cut seven strips 2½in wide across the width of the fabric.

Seam allowance:
- Use scant ¼in seams throughout.

Making the Half-square Triangle Units

1. Refer to the instructions for making half-square triangle units on page 10 and layer a dark and light fat quarter.

2. You only need to cut nine squares from each fat quarter, so cut three strips each 5⅜in wide and then sub-cut each strip into three squares each 5⅜in x 5⅜in.

3. Repeat with the other dark and light fat quarters. You need fifty-two half-square triangles in total (two are spare).

Assembling your Quilt

- Lay out all your light and dark charm squares in fourteen rows of fourteen (see diagram below for placing the squares and half-square triangles).
- When you are happy with the layout, label the first square of each row with the row number, to ensure they stay in the correct order after sewing.
- Sew the squares into rows and then join the rows together, pinning at every intersection to ensure a perfect match. Press the work.
- Your quilt top is now complete. Quilt as desired and bind to finish (see page 124).

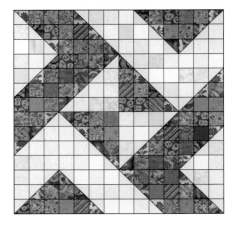

opposite:
Charisma by Chez Moi gave us just the colourwash effect we wanted for this quilt. We chose a distinctive quilting design called 'Splat' – a fun design for a fun quilt. The quilt was pieced by the authors and longarm quilted by The Quilt Room.

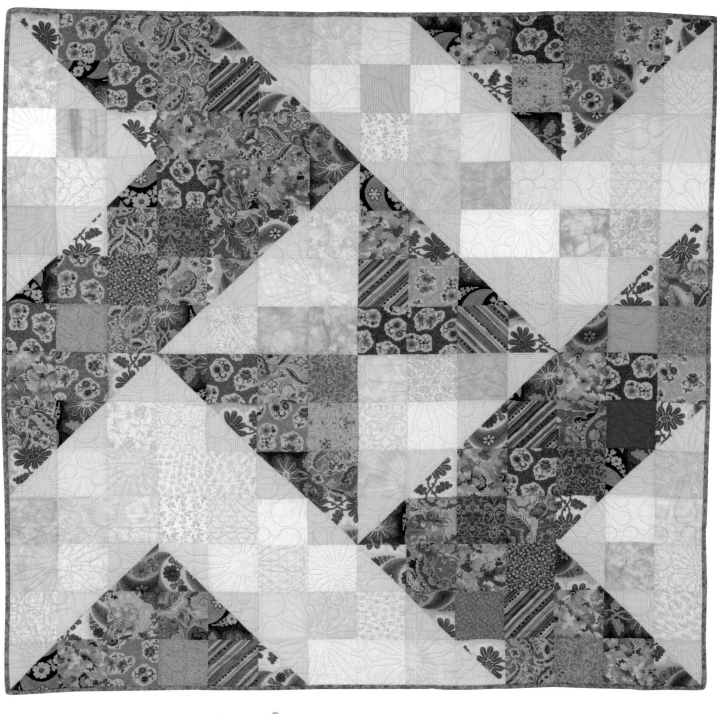

Raspberry Ripple

Vital statistics

Quilt size:	64in x 80in
Block size:	12in
Number of blocks:	32
Setting:	blocks on point

The nine-patch block works so well with a jelly roll. You can make sixty nine-patch blocks quickly from just one jelly roll. Nine-patch blocks can be mixed with many other blocks to create stunning quilts; we put two in our previous book – one mixed with the hourglass block and the other with a snowball block. This pattern does something completely different with the nine-patch block until it becomes virtually unrecognisable.

When devising the pattern, the quilt lent itself to being set five blocks by six blocks, which would have used up all the blocks with very little wastage. It did look good but we kept looking at the quilt diagonally and couldn't help preferring it that way. To set the quilt on point meant that we needed to make up two more blocks. Luckily our offcuts from making the nine-patch blocks came into their own. We sewed them up to make scrappy nine-patch blocks, which meant we had sufficient blocks and absolutely no wastage.

We used a red jelly roll with a cream background and chose red setting triangles, which we cut on the large side to make the pattern 'float'. We were delighted with our 'much larger than planned' quilt!

What you need

- One jelly roll **or** forty 2½in strips cut across the width of the fabric
- 2¼yd (2m) background fabric
- 1½yd (1.4m) fabric for setting triangles
- 24in (60cm) fabric for binding

opposite:
This quilt would not be easily recognized as being made from a nine-patch block but that is how it started out! We thought the quilt looked very romantic so we decided upon a heart design for the quilting. The quilt was pieced by the authors and longarm quilted by The Quilt Room.

Cutting Instructions

Background fabric:
- Cut eleven 6½in strips across the width of the fabric.
- Sub-cut each strip into six squares 6½in x 6½in. You need sixty-four in total (two are spare).

Setting triangles:
- Cut two strips 19in wide across the width of the fabric. Sub-cut each into two squares 19in x 19in.
- Cut across both diagonals of each square to create sixteen setting triangles (two are spare).
- Cut one strip 11in across the fabric width. Sub-cut this strip into two squares 11in x 11in.
- Cut across one diagonal of each square to create four corner triangles. Cutting the setting and corner triangles in this way ensures that there are no bias edges on the outside of your quilt.

Binding fabric:
- Cut eight 2½in wide strips across the width of fabric.

Seam allowance:
- Use scant ¼in seams throughout.

Making the Nine-patch Blocks

1. Pair up the forty jelly roll strips. Take one pair and trim the selvedge. Cut each into three lengths of approximately 14in. From your six lengths assemble two-strip segments. Press seams to the darker fabric.

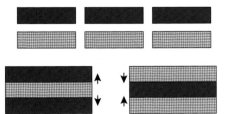

2. Now cut each into five 2½in segments.

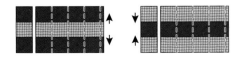

3. Assemble and sew the three nine-patch blocks as shown in the diagrams below, pinning at every intersection to make sure that the seams are neatly aligned. Press and put the spare unit to one side.

4. Repeat with other sets of strips to make sixty nine-patch blocks.

5. Choose twelve of the spare units and make up four more scrappy nine-patch blocks. You need sixty-four nine-patch blocks in total.

6. Take one of the 6½in background squares and on the wrong side draw a line across one of the diagonals.

7. With right sides together, lay the marked background square on top of one of the nine-patch blocks, aligning the edges. Sew a ¼in seam on both sides of the marked diagonal.

8. Press the stitching line to set the stitches. Cut the units apart between the stitching, cutting on the marked line. Trim the dog ears and press open towards the background fabric to create two new units.

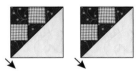

9. Using a quilting square, trim the units to measure 6in square. Make sure the diagonal markings on the quilting square align with the diagonal of the unit. You will need to trim two sides and then rotate the square to trim the other two sides. Repeat with the remaining sixty-three background

and nine-patch units to create a total of 128 units.

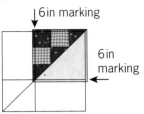

Assembling the Blocks

1. The quilt is made up of two different blocks, both formed from four of the units – a pinwheel (below left) and a diamond (below right).

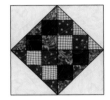
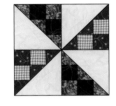

Pinwheel block   Diamond block

2. Make up twenty pinwheel blocks and twelve diamond blocks, pinning at every intersection to ensure a perfect fit. They can be as scrappy or as coordinated as you like. Press, trying to ensure that you are pressing seams in different directions to create less bulk.

Setting Blocks on Point

1. Referring to the diagram below, sew a setting triangle to each side of a pinwheel block to create Row 1. The setting triangles have been cut slightly larger to make the blocks 'float', so when sewing the setting triangles make sure that the bottom of the triangle is aligned with the block. Press seams as shown in the diagram below.

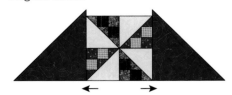

2. Following the diagram (right), continue to sew the blocks together to form rows with setting triangles at each end. Pin at every intersection to ensure a perfect match. Press, trying to ensure that you are pressing the seams in different directions on alternate rows so that seams nest together nicely.

3. Sew the rows together, pinning at every intersection, and sew the corner triangles on last.

Finishing the Quilt

Your quilt top is now complete. Quilt as desired and bind to finish (see page 124).

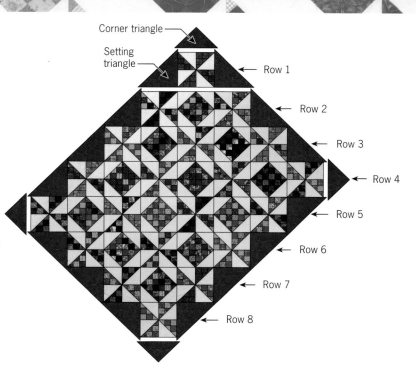

Corner triangle

Setting triangle

Row 1
Row 2
Row 3
Row 4
Row 5
Row 6
Row 7
Row 8

Blossom Time

Vital statistics

Quilt size:	58in x 69in
Block size:	9in
Number of blocks:	20
Setting:	4 x 5 blocks
	plus 6in border

The range of fabrics used in this quilt is called Cottage Romance from Maywood Studios and has just the right mix of colours to create a cottage garden. We fell in love with the border fabric and the quilt just fell into place – you could say it grew! We used charm packs from the Cottage Romance range but this quilt would look great in any mix of colours. The variation on page 23 shows how this design would look in rich, earthy tones.

If you have a favourite fabric in your stash that you love so much you are reluctant to cut it up, how about working this quilt around it? Just two charm packs, a fat quarter and some sashing fabric are all that is needed to add to your border. As we loved the border so much (and not to be wasteful with any of it) we also made the binding from it. Our quilting design of butterflies flying around the garden added the final touch.

What you need

- Two charm packs **or** eighty squares 5in x 5in
- One fat quarter for flower centres
- 1¾yd (1.6m) fabric for sashing and inner border
- 1¾yd (1.6m) fabric for outer border and binding

opposite:
Having such a beautiful large floral design for the border we didn't want any joins to show so we made sure that we had sufficient fabric to cut the borders in one length. Now you know us well enough by now to realize that we wouldn't be wasteful, especially with such gorgeous fabric, so we cut our binding from it as well. A butterfly quilting design added the final touch. The quilt was pieced by the authors and longarm quilted by The Quilt Room.

Cutting Instructions

Sashing and inner border:

- Cut this fabric lengthways so you will not need to have any joins.
- Fold lengthways aligning the selvedge and cut fifteen strips 2½in wide.
- Put eight strips aside for sashing strips to be trimmed later.
- Sub-cut three strips into fifteen rectangles 2½in x 9½in.
- Sub-cut four strips into eighty squares 2½in x 2½in. These are the large flip-over corner squares.

> **tip**
>
> You can fold the fabric lengthways more than once to make it easier to cut but *do* open out your first strip after cutting to check that the folds are not causing any zigzags. If there are any zigzags, it means you need to re-straighten your cutting edge.

Flower centre:

- Cut the fat quarter into seven strips 1½in wide and sub-cut each strip into twelve squares 1½in x 1½in. You need eighty in total.

Outer border and binding:

- Cut four strips lengthways 6½in wide.
- Cut four strips lengthways 2½in wide.

Seam allowance:

- Use scant ¼in seams throughout.

Sewing the Flowers

1. Take one 2½in x 2½in square and lay it right sides together on a 5in charm square as shown in the diagram below.

2. For the first few squares, draw a diagonal line or make a crease in the fabric to mark the sewing line but after sewing a few you will probably find it unnecessary. Sew across the diagonal.

3. Repeat until you have all of the 2½in squares sewn to a charm square. Chain piecing speeds up this process – see diagram below and also page 123.

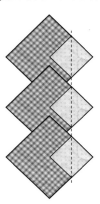

4. Press the 2½in squares towards the outer edge as shown below. Trim the excess from the 2½in square but do not trim the charm square. Although this creates a little more bulk, keeping the charm square uncut will keep your unit in shape.

5. Take one flower centre square and lay it right sides together on a 5in charm square as shown below.

> **tip**
>
> When sewing on a flip-and-sew corner, instead of sewing along the marked diagonal line or crease, sew a thread width to the right and your corner will fit better when flipped over.

6. For the first few squares, draw a diagonal line or make a crease in the fabric to mark the sewing line but after sewing a few you will probably find it unnecessary. Sew across the diagonal.

7. Repeat until you have all the flower centres sewn to a charm square. Chain piecing speeds up this process.

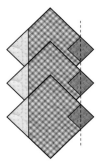

8. Press the flower centres towards the outer edge. Once pressed and you can see that your flower centres are properly aligned, trim *both* the excess flower centre and the charm square excess to reduce bulk when joining the flower centres.

9. Sort the charm squares into groups of four. In our main quilt we kept the same colours together but in our variation on page 23 we made it scrappier. When you have decided which pairs are to be sewn together, press one of the flower centre seams in each pair in the *other* direction, to create less bulk in the centre.

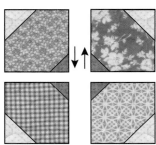

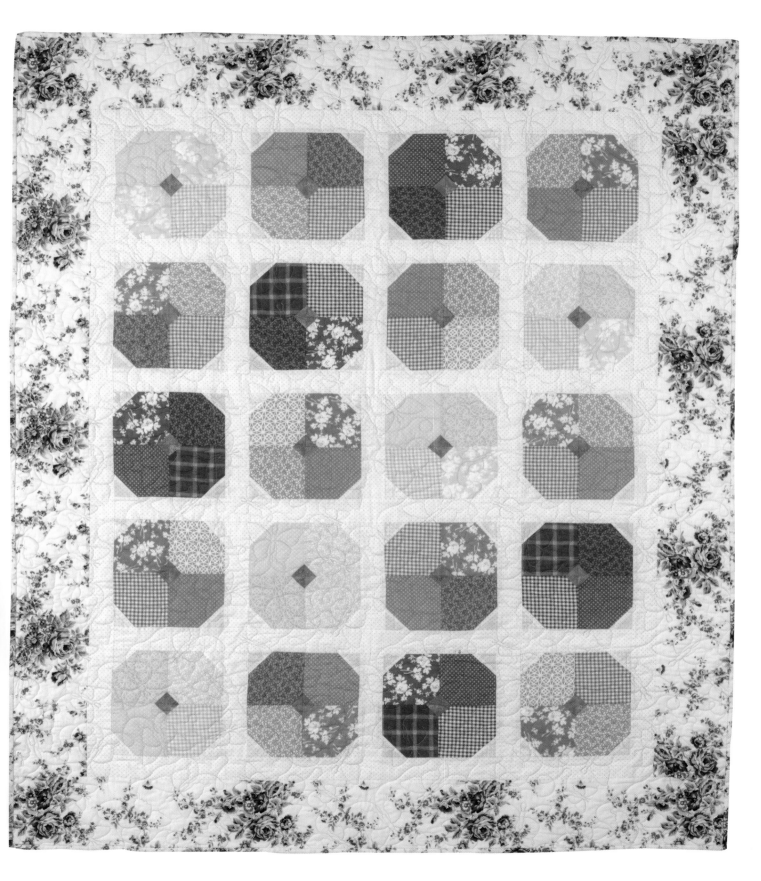

tip

When changing the direction of a pressed seam, always press it back to its original position before re-pressing the other way.

Adding the Sashing Strips and Inner Border

1. Lay out your blocks and once you are happy with the layout, sew a 2½in x 9½in sashing strip to the right-hand side of the first three blocks in row 1 (see diagram below). Do not sew a sashing strip to the block on the right.

2. Sew the blocks together to form row 1 and press. Repeat to make five rows in total.

3. Measure your rows carefully and trim the six horizontal sashings to this measurement. They must all be the same length in order to keep the quilt square. Sew rows and horizontal sashing strips together and then press.

4. Measure the quilt from top to bottom to get the vertical measurement. Trim the two remaining sashing strips to this measurement. Pin and sew to the quilt and then press.

10. Sew the pairs together, pinning at the seams to ensure a perfect match. Press the work in the direction shown.

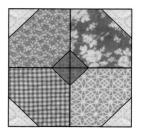

11. Sew one pair to the other pair to form the flower, pinning at the seams to ensure a perfect match. Press the work.

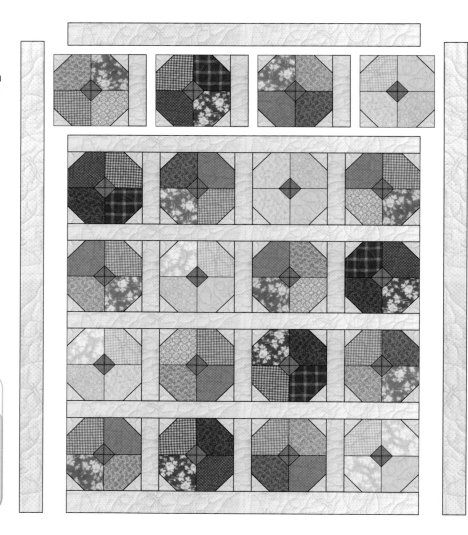

tip

When joining the sashing to a row, mark the centre of both the sashing strip and the row and pin in position. Now pin at both ends and continue pinning in position, easing if necessary.

Sewing your Outer Borders

- Determine the vertical measurement from top to bottom through the centre of your quilt top. Trim the two side borders to this measurement (see diagram right). Sew to the quilt. Press out to the borders.
- Determine the horizontal measurement from side to side across the centre of the quilt top. Trim these two borders to this measurement. Sew the borders to the quilt and press.
- Your quilt top is now complete. Quilt as desired and then bind (see page 124).

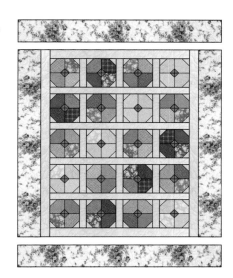

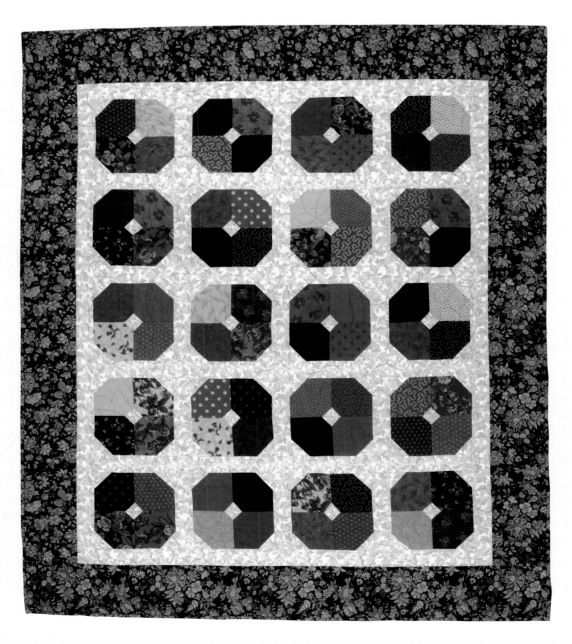

Our variation uses Moda's reproduction fabrics Renewal from Brannock & Patek. We mixed the fabrics around to create a much more scrappy quilt. It just shows how different a quilt can look made up with different fabrics and there is always a fabric range out there to suit everyone! The quilt was pieced by the authors and longarm quilted by The Quilt Room.

Diamonds at Large

Vital statistics

Quilt size: 45in x 60in
Block Size: 6¾in x 9¼in
Number of blocks: 36
Setting: 6 x 6 blocks plus 2in border

The original idea for this quilt was to have a diamond centre in a medallion quilt and to use a jelly roll for the outside borders. However, once we had made the quilt centre we liked it just as it was and felt it wouldn't be enhanced with intricate borders. If we wanted a larger quilt, we decided it would be better to just have more diamonds!

We sorted the cut off rectangles into lights and darks. Then we made the lights into a border and the darks into a binding – the result of this is a fabulous diamond quilt that didn't cost a fortune.

The range that we have used is Fig Tree's Fig and Plum, which had a good selection of lights. We were a couple short but didn't want to compromise the design by using anything too dark in the background. We had a light fat quarter from the same range so we cut two 10in squares from that to add to our lights.

From a fat quarter you can cut two strips 2½in wide, which is equal to one jelly roll strip, and two 10in squares, which is equal to two layers of layer cake. So, from a bundle of forty fat quarters you can make one jelly roll and two layer cakes – that's got to be useful to know.

The variation on page 29 features small-scale floral taupes and the design works well with larger-scale prints too.

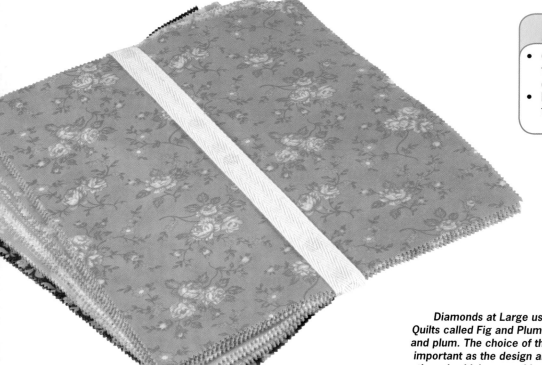

What you need

- One layer cake **or** forty 10in squares (at least eighteen light and eighteen dark)
- Border and binding fabric is cut from the layer cake

opposite:
***Diamonds at Large** uses the gorgeous range from **Fig Tree Quilts** called **Fig and Plum** – such a lovely mix of peach, cream and plum. The choice of the quilting thread colour is equally as important as the design and for this quilt we chose a soft aqua thread, which created just the effect we wanted. The quilt was pieced by the authors and longarm quilted by **The Quilt Room**.*

Cutting Instructions

Layer cake:

- Rotary cut thirty-six of your 10in squares into two rectangles: one 2½in x 10in and one 7½in x 10in (see diagram below). Put the 2½in x 10in strips aside for the border and binding, together with the remaining four layer cake squares.

Seam allowance:

- Use scant ¼in seams throughout.

tip

Take care when dealing with bias edges – try not to pull them about too much or they may stretch.

Sewing the Blocks

1. Sort the 7½in x 10in rectangles into lights and darks – you need eighteen light and eighteen dark. This design really does need a distinction between the two.

2. Make a stack of six of the 7½in x 10in rectangles, all right sides up, alternating dark and light squares and aligning the edges, and then press.

3. Rotary cut a diagonal line across the rectangle stack from the bottom right to the top left corner (see diagram below).

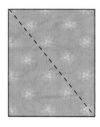

4. Take the top right triangle and put it at the bottom of the pile (see below). This changes the order so that your top two triangles are now a dark and a light.

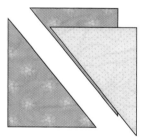

5. With right sides together, sew the top dark and light triangles together to form a rectangle (below, left). This is a bias edge so do not pull the fabric too much. Trim the dog ears and press open to the dark fabric (see below, right). Continue through the stack forming rectangles from the triangles. Repeat with two more stacks of six rectangles. You need eighteen rectangles with the diagonal in this direction and with seams pressed to the dark fabric.

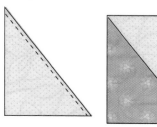

6. Repeat the procedure with the other eighteen 7½in x 10in rectangles but, *importantly*, you now need to cut the diagonal in the *other* direction from bottom left to top right (see diagram below, left). Take the top left triangle and put it at the bottom of the pile (see diagram below, right) to change the order of the fabrics.

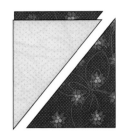

7. With right sides together, sew the top dark and light triangles together to form a rectangle, taking care with the bias edge. Continue through the stack. Trim the dog ears and press open to the light fabric (see diagram below).

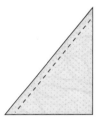

8. You now have eighteen rectangles with the diagonal in one direction and the seams pressed to the dark fabric and eighteen with the diagonal in the other direction and the seams pressed to the light fabric.

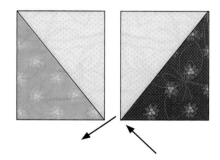

Sewing the Blocks Together

1. Referring to the diagram right, lay out your blocks and when you are happy with the layout, sew four blocks into a diamond, as shown below, pinning at the seam intersections to ensure a perfect match. Press the work.

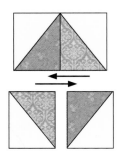

2. Repeat with the other rectangles until you have nine diamond blocks.

3. Sew the diamond blocks into rows, as shown in the diagram, right, and then sew the rows together, pinning at the intersections to ensure a perfect match.

4. Now join the three rows of three diamonds together to form the centre of the quilt.

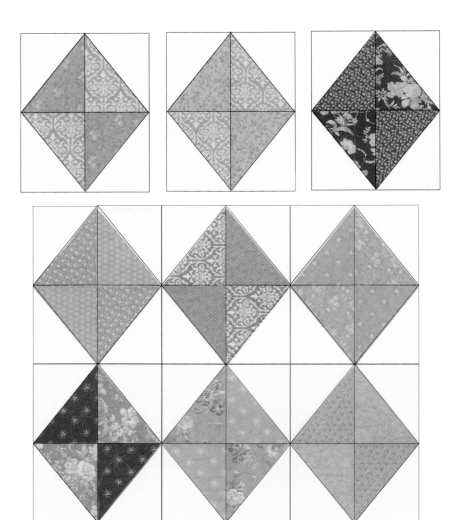

tip

Keep your sewing at a constant speed. Sewing too fast can produce uneven stitches so a steady pace is preferable and will result in much neater work.

Sewing your Borders

- Cut each of the four spare layer cakes into 2½in strips and add these to the thirty-six 2½in x 10in strips from the other layer cakes, which you have put aside for the border and binding. You need forty-eight in total.
- Select twenty-two of the lightest for the border. Sew two lengths of six for the side borders and two lengths of five for the top and bottom borders (see diagram left).
- Determine the vertical measurement, from top to bottom through the centre of your quilt top. Trim the two side borders to this measurement. Sew to the quilt and press.
- Determine the horizontal measurement, from side to side across the centre of the quilt top. Trim these two borders to this measurement. Sew to the quilt and press.
- Sew the remaining twenty-four 2½in x 10in strips into a continuous length ready for binding your quilt.
- Your quilt top is now complete. Quilt as desired and bind to finish (see page 124).

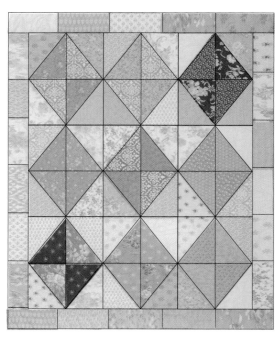

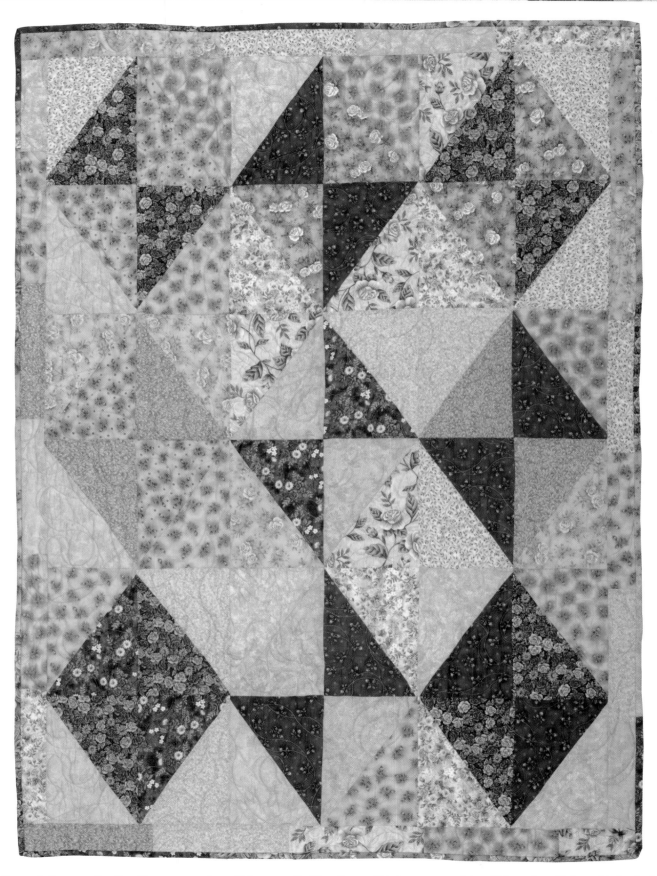

Our variation uses the floral taupe range from Makower called Zen Roses. This is a super-quick quilt to make which would also look great with those large-scale prints you want to show off. The quilt was pieced by the authors and longarm quilted by The Quilt Room.

High-Flying Geese

Vital statistics

Quilt size:	44in x 68in
Block size:	8in
Number of blocks:	40
Setting:	5 x 8 blocks
	plus 2in border

Heather Bailey's fabrics look good in any quilt but we especially love the way that they sparkle here. This is a very simple traditional block sometimes known as Dutchman's Puzzle. The flying geese units fly off in different directions to create the lively twirling effect.

Don't be daunted by the number of little squares and rectangles as once you get chain piecing it really does go together quickly. There is absolutely no wastage as the offcuts from the jelly roll strips are used to make the border.

In our variation, shown on page 35, instead of using the offcuts for the border we chose to use them for our binding and inserted a 6in wide border made from the background blue fabric. This border required an extra 1⅓yd (1.25m), cut into six strips 6½in wide, and it enlarged the quilt to 56in x 80in. So keep an open mind when choosing how to finish your quilt.

What you need

- One jelly roll **or**
  forty 2½in strips cut across the width of the fabric
- 3yd (2.75m) background fabric
- 20in (50cm) fabric for binding
  Note: if you choose to have a 6in wide border and use your jelly roll strips for binding, as we did in our variation, you will need 1⅓yd (1.25m) of border fabric cut into six 6½in wide strips across the width of the fabric and you won't need any binding fabric

opposite:
Large, bold designs are often avoided when you know that you will be cutting small pieces but we love the fact that cutting up a large design creates so many different effects. The quilt was pieced by the authors and longarm quilted by The Quilt Room.

Cutting Instructions

Jelly roll strips:

- Cut each strip into eight rectangles 2½in x 4½in. Once you have cut the eight rectangles, keep them together in a pile. You need a total of 320 rectangles. The balance of the strip (approximately 6in) will be used for the border.

  Note: if you are cutting your strips folded, make sure that you start cutting from the selvedge end so your excess fabric will be in one piece.

Background fabric:

- Cut forty 2½in strips across the width of the fabric.

> **tip**
>
> When cutting strips, don't be tempted to stack too many as you will lose accuracy. It is better to have smaller stacks but line them up next to each other so that you can cut more than one strip at a time.

- Sub-cut each strip into sixteen 2½in squares. You need 640 in total. Any excess fabric may be used to add to your border, if required.

Binding fabric:

- Cut six 2½in wide strips across the width of fabric.

Seam allowance:

- Use scant ¼in seams throughout.

Sewing the Flying Geese Units

1. Choose two piles of rectangles that look good together. Take one background 2½in square and lay it right sides together on a 2½in x 4½in jelly roll rectangle. Sew across the diagonal as shown in the diagram below. You may choose to draw the diagonal line in first to mark your stitching line but after sewing a few, you will probably find it unnecessary. Flip the square over and press towards the background fabric. Trim the excess background fabric but do not trim the jelly roll fabric. Although this creates a little more bulk, this will keep your flying geese in shape.

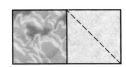

2. Place a second background 2½in square and lay it on the other side as shown below and sew across the diagonal. Flip the square over and press. Trim the excess background fabric.

3. Repeat with all the rectangles from the two strips to make sixteen units.

Note: if you really don't like having the extra bulk and want to trim the jelly roll fabric as well as the background fabric, it is *imperative* that you ensure your units are correct before cutting. If they are not accurate and you don't have the jelly roll fabric to guide you, your flying geese will be flying in all directions!

4. Sew a Flying Geese unit from each strip together as shown in the diagram below. The fabric on the right of the unit will form the centre of the block so you can choose which one you want to place there. Press as shown. Repeat to form eight units.

  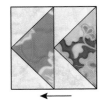

5. Assemble the block as shown in the diagram below. Press as shown. Make two of these blocks. Repeat with your other jelly roll strips to make a total of forty blocks.

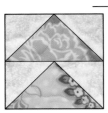 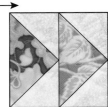

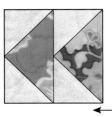 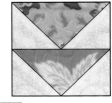

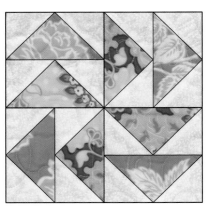

> **tip**
>
> Don't be daunted by the number of rectangles and squares to be sewn. Once you know what you are doing you can get into a system of chain piecing and it goes together quickly.

Sewing your Blocks Together

- Referring to the diagram, right, join the blocks together, five blocks across and eight blocks down, pinning at every intersection to ensure a perfect match. Press when finished.

Sewing your Borders

- Join your offcuts from the jelly roll strips into a continuous length. You need at least 220in. If you have less than this, use some of your excess background fabric cut into 2½in strips.
- Determine the vertical measurement from top to bottom through the centre of your quilt top. Trim the two side borders to this measurement. Sew to the quilt and then press.
- Determine the horizontal measurement from side to side across the centre of the quilt top. Trim these two borders to this measurement. Sew to the quilt.
- Your quilt top is now complete. Quilt as desired and bind to finish (see page 124).

Our variation shows just how lovely 1930s fabrics can look when mixed with a thirties blue. We often mix our thirties fabrics with a crisp white background, which sets off the colourful fabrics, but if you feel like something different try a lovely soft blue. In this variation we also added a 6in wide border; for this an extra $1\frac{1}{3}$yd (1.25m) was required, cut into six strips 6½in wide. We then used our offcuts for the binding. We hope this gives you ideas for different ways on how you can individualize your quilt. The quilt was pieced by the authors and longarm quilted by The Quilt Room in a thirties floral design.

Old Gold

Late one night we were frantically trying to complete this quilt because we were intrigued to know whether there would be sufficient scraps left over to create the binding. Eventually, when we had finished sewing all the scraps together we discovered that we had *just* enough – less than a 10in strip remaining – so just remember when you are trimming your selvedges not to waste any fabric and you might have enough for your binding as well! The end result was a double quilt measuring 72 x 80in including border and binding – all from one jelly roll and one layer cake.

The variation shown on page 41 uses a fresh, spring-like mix of pinks, greens and yellows.

What you need

- One jelly roll and one layer cake **or** forty 2½in strips cut across the width of the fabric and forty 10in squares
- 24in (60cm) of fabric for binding, cut into eight 2½in wide strips the width of fabric (or use offcuts as we did)

opposite:
We used Harvest Home by Blackbird designs for the jelly roll and layer cake. The hourglass blocks were made from the layer cake and the sashings, border and binding came from the jelly roll. The two log cabin blocks also came from the jelly roll – an attractive feature that added to the design of the quilt.

Sewing the Two Log Cabin Blocks

This quilt requires forty-two blocks but you can only make forty from the 10in squares in your layer cake. However, you do have lots of strip offcuts plus three complete strips giving you enough to make up two Log Cabin blocks, which we placed on two of the diagonals.

1. Take a small 2½in wide strip of fabric of your choice, at least 2½in long (the first log), and a 1½in centre square. With right sides together, sew them together. Press away from centre (see diagram below). It does feel a little strange with a centre square smaller than the strip but this will give you the required size of log cabin block and it looks effective. Trim the log to size.

1½in wide centre

2½in wide log

2. Choose another strip of fabric in similar colouring (the second log) and sew to this unit. Press to the outer log (see below). Trim the log to size.

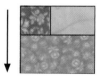

3. Choose a strip of a different colour (the third log) and sew to this unit. Press to outer log (see below). Trim the log to size.

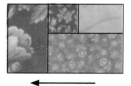

4. Choose another strip of fabric in similar colouring (the fourth log) and sew to this unit. Press to the outer log (see below). Trim the log to size.

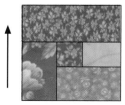

5. Repeat the previous steps to sew another round of logs, trimming to size as you go (see below). Press to the outer logs. Your finished block will now be 9in. Make two log cabin blocks.

Sewing your Sashing Strips

1. Take forty-eight of the 2½in x 9in rectangles and sew a dark 2½in square to one end, as shown in the diagram below. Press as shown.

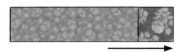

2. Take eight of these and sew another 2½in dark square to the other end, as shown below. Press as shown.

Assembling your Blocks

- Referring to the diagram below lay out the blocks with the sashing strips in between. Make seven rows of six blocks.
- When you are happy with the layout, sew the sashing strips to the blocks as shown, pinning at every seam intersection to ensure a perfect match. Press the vertical sashing strips towards the hourglass blocks and your seams will nest together nicely. Now sew the rows together.

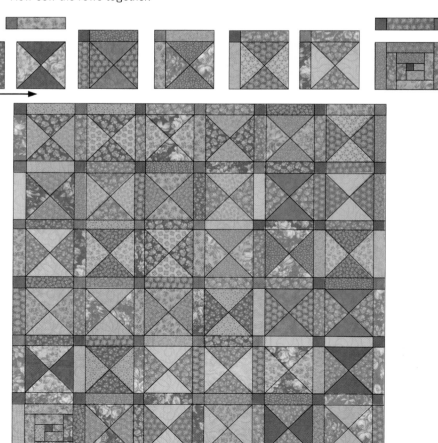

Adding your Borders

- Join two of the border strips together to form a longer length. Repeat this with the remaining border strips.

- Now follow the directions on page 123 for sewing on the borders.
- Your quilt top is now complete. Quilt as desired and bind to finish (see page 124).

Now follow the directions on page 123 for sewing on the borders.

tip

You need about 310in for binding your quilt and you should have sufficient but it depends on how much selvedge you needed to trim. Chain piece all your different lengths together to form one continuous 2½in wide strip. Not only will you be using every last scrap but the scrappy binding is the perfect finishing touch.

Here is the same quilt looking very spring-like in the latest April Cornell range called Spring Magic, which has a gorgeous mix of pinks and greens. The quilt was pieced by the authors and longarm quilted by The Quilt Room.

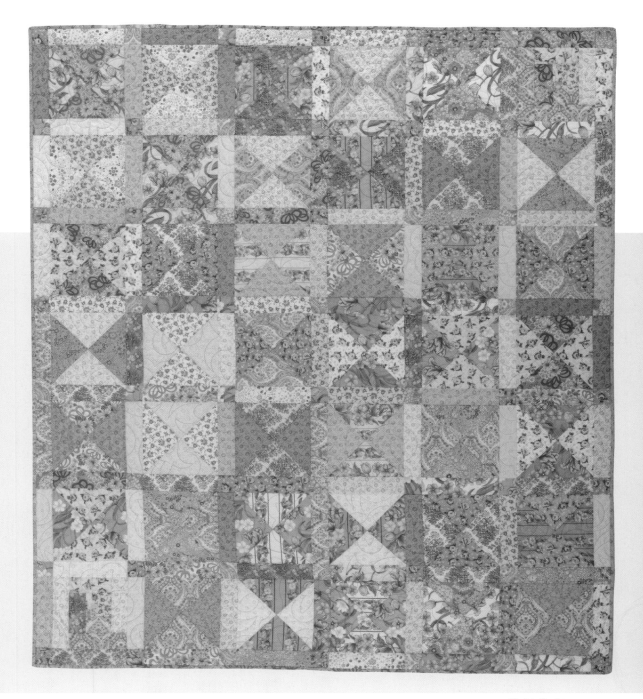

Hidden Stars

Vital statistics

Quilt size:	59in x 72in
Block size:	9in
	with 4½in sashing
Number of blocks:	20
Setting:	4 x 5 blocks

Just like magic, a star appears when the blocks in this quilt are sewn together! This gentle floral range combined with a white on white fabric creates a stunning quilt to grace a country cottage or stately home. This quilt really would look good anywhere.

The quilt is quick and easy to put together so it's definitely a pattern to remember for a hurried gift or when you need to create something fast.

Just to show how totally different this quilt can look, our variation shown on page 47 is made with the Barbara Brackman range called Civil War Crossing. We loved the fact that there were so many pinks in it and we chose our stars to be a lovely deep red.

What you need

- One layer cake **or** forty 10in squares
- 1yd (1m) of fabric for the stars
- 20in (50cm) fabric for binding

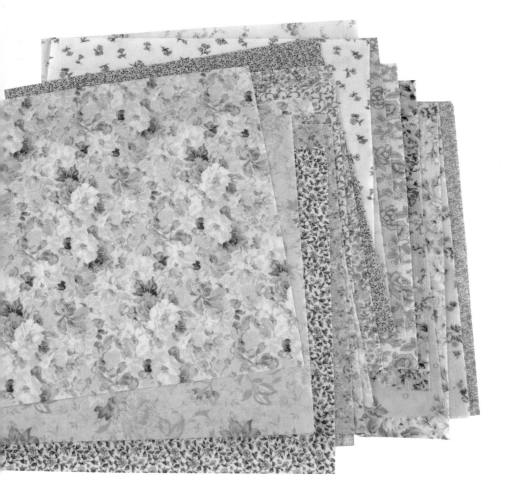

opposite:
__Hidden Stars__ uses a floral layer cake that is full of country charm. It would look stunning thrown over a chair to bring a small part of the garden into the home. The quilt was pieced by the authors and longarm quilted by The Quilt Room in a simple flower design.

Cutting Instructions

The 10in squares:
- Cut each square into two rectangles each 5in x 10in.
- Cut one rectangle in half to make two squares 5in x 5in. You need eighty of these squares.
- Trim the other rectangle to 5in x 9½in. You only need thirty-one of these rectangles and so will have nine spare.

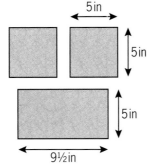

Star fabric:
- Cut nine strips 2¾in wide across the width of the fabric.
- Sub-cut each strip into fourteen squares 2¾in x 2¾in. You need 124.
- Cut two strips 5in wide across the width of the fabric.
- Sub-cut each strip into six squares 5in x 5in. You need twelve.

Binding fabric:
- Cut seven strips 2½in wide across the width of the fabric.

Seam allowance:
- Use scant ¼in seams throughout.

Sewing the Four-Patch Blocks

1. Take two floral 5in squares and, with right sides together, sew down one side with a scant ¼in seam allowance (see diagram below). Continue chain piecing until you have sewn all your pairs of 5in floral squares together. You will have forty pairs. Don't worry too much about the selection of the squares but avoid sewing two of the same squares together.

2. Snip between pairs and press each paired unit towards the darker fabric.

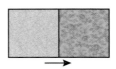

3. Pair up the units and turn one round so that the darker fabric is next to the lighter on the other unit. Pin at seam intersections to ensure a perfect match. Sew down one side with a scant ¼in seam allowance (see below). Continue chain piecing until you have sewn all your paired units together.

4. Snip between the paired units and press open. You will have twenty four-patch blocks.

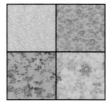

Sewing the Sashing Rectangles

1. Take a 2¾in star square and draw a diagonal line from corner to corner on the wrong side of the fabric.

2. With right sides together, lay a marked square on one corner of a 5in x 9½in rectangle, aligning the outer edges (see below). Sew across the diagonal using the marked diagonal line as the stitching line. After a while you may find you don't need to draw the line as it's not difficult to judge the sewing line. Alternatively, fold the square diagonally before sewing so you have a faint crease to act as the stitching line.

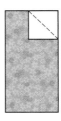

3. Open the square out and press towards the outside of the block, aligning the raw edges. Fold the corner back down and trim the excess star fabric ¼in beyond the stitching line *but do not trim the rectangle*. Although this creates a little more bulk, this rectangle will keep your work in shape.

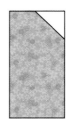

4. Trim the corner and press. Repeat with the square on the other side.

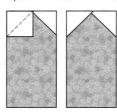

5. Repeat with the other two corners, as shown. Repeat this with the other rectangle. You need thirty-one in total.

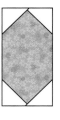

Assembling the Blocks

1. Create Row 1 by sewing a sashing rectangle to the right-hand side of three selected four-patch blocks and adding a four-patch block to the right-hand side of the last sashing rectangle (see diagrams below). Press as shown. Repeat to create four more rows the same as Row 1.

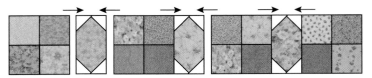

2. Create Row 2 by sewing a 5in star square to the right-hand side of a sashing rectangle and adding a sashing rectangle to the right-hand side of the last star square.

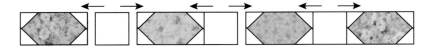

Press as shown above. Repeat to create three more rows the same as Row 2.

3. Referring to the diagram below, sew the rows together, alternating the rows. Pin at every seam intersection before sewing to ensure the perfect match.

4. Your quilt top is now complete. Quilt as desired and bind to finish (see page 124).

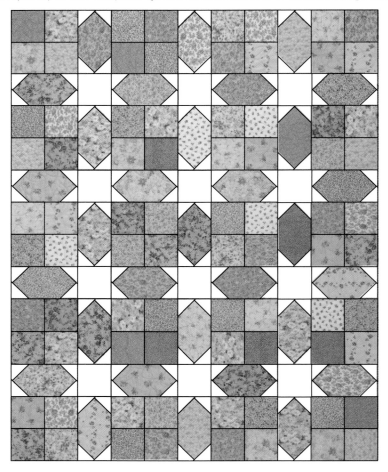

Our variation is made with the Barbara Brackman range of reproduction American Civil War fabrics called Civil War Crossing. We loved the fact that there were so many pinks in it and we chose our stars to be a deep red. If the range you are using does not contain so many of the gorgeous pinks, you could of course choose to have your stars in a reproduction pink fabric.

Damask Rose

Vital statistics

Quilt size:	50in x 62in
Block size:	10in
Number of blocks:	20
Setting:	4 x 5 blocks with 2in sashing

What you need

- One jelly roll **or** forty 2½in strips cut across the width of the fabric
- Four coordinating fat quarters for sashing strips (if you don't want such a scrappy effect for the sashing you can use 1yd/1m of a fabric)
- 20in (50cm) of fabric for binding
- Omnigrid 96 triangular ruler (or similar)

When thinking of a name for this pretty quilt that was made from the Mary Rose fabrics by Quilt Gate, we started researching the meaning behind the number of roses that are sent in a bouquet. Our quilt has twenty rose blocks, and we discovered that giving twenty roses represents 'Believe me, I am sincere towards you'. You don't have to read any message into our quilt – just enjoy the beautiful fabrics.

The vintage fabrics in delicate pinks, creams, blues and beiges, blend together beautifully and create a quilt with a timeless quality. Our dense feather-pattern quilting gives the quilt an added dimension and texture.

This quilt uses the Omnigrid 96 triangular ruler to make the half-square triangles. If you are using a different type of ruler, please ensure that you are using the correct markings.

opposite:
Damask Rose uses the antique floral fabrics from Quilt Gate called Mary Rose. We chose a dense feather quilting design which gives the quilt texture and an added dimension. The quilt was pieced by the authors and longarm quilted by The Quilt Room.

Sorting your Strips

- Sort your jelly roll strips into pairs that look good together and allocate one to be Fabric A and the other Fabric B.
- Each of these pairs will make one block: Fabric A will be used for the centres and outside of the block and Fabric B will form the star.

Cutting Instructions

Jelly roll:
- Cut your Fabric A strips as follows:
  – one rectangle 2½in x 6½in
  – six squares 2½in x 2½in
  – one rectangle 2½in x 15in.
- Cut your Fabric B strips as follows:
  – ten squares 2½in x 2½in (set two from each strip aside for sashing squares)
  – one rectangle 2½in x 15in.

Sashing:
- Press your four fat quarters, trim selvedge and cut each one into seven 2½in strips as shown below. **It is important** to make sure you cut them so that each strip measures at least 21in. Sub-cut each strip into two 2½in x 10½in rectangles. You need forty-nine of these sashing strips.

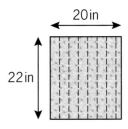

Binding:
- Cut into six 2½in wide strips across the width of the fabric.

Seam allowance:
- Use scant ¼in seams throughout.

Making the Half-Square Triangle Units

1. Take a pair of the Fabric A and Fabric B 2½in x 15in rectangles and press right sides together, ensuring that they are exactly one on top of the other. The pressing will help hold the two strips together.

2. Lay out on a cutting mat and trim the selvedge on the left side. Position the Omnigrid 96 as shown in diagram below, lining up the 2in mark at the bottom edge of the strips and cut the first triangle. You will notice that the cut out triangle has a flat top. This would just have been a dog ear you needed to cut off, so it is saving you time!

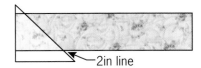

3. Rotate the ruler 180 degrees to the right as shown below and cut the next triangle. Continue in this way along the strip. You need eight sets of triangles from each pair of strips.

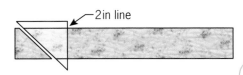

4. Sew along the diagonals to form eight half-square triangles. Trim all dog ears and press open.

5. Repeat with all the Fabric A and the Fabric B 2½in x 15in rectangles.

Sewing each Block

1. Making Unit 1: sew a Fabric A square to a Fabric B square to form Unit 1. Make two of these units. Press seams as shown.

2. Making Unit 2: sew a Fabric B square to either end of a Fabric A 2½in x 6½in rectangle to form Unit 2. Press seams as shown below.

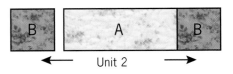

tip

Before sewing your blocks together it is a good idea to make twenty separate piles for each block so you don't mix up the fabrics. Each pile should contain:
Fabric A – one 2½in x 6½in rectangle
Fabric A – six 2½in x 2½in squares
Fabric B – eight 2½in x 2½in squares
Fabric A & B – eight half-square triangle units

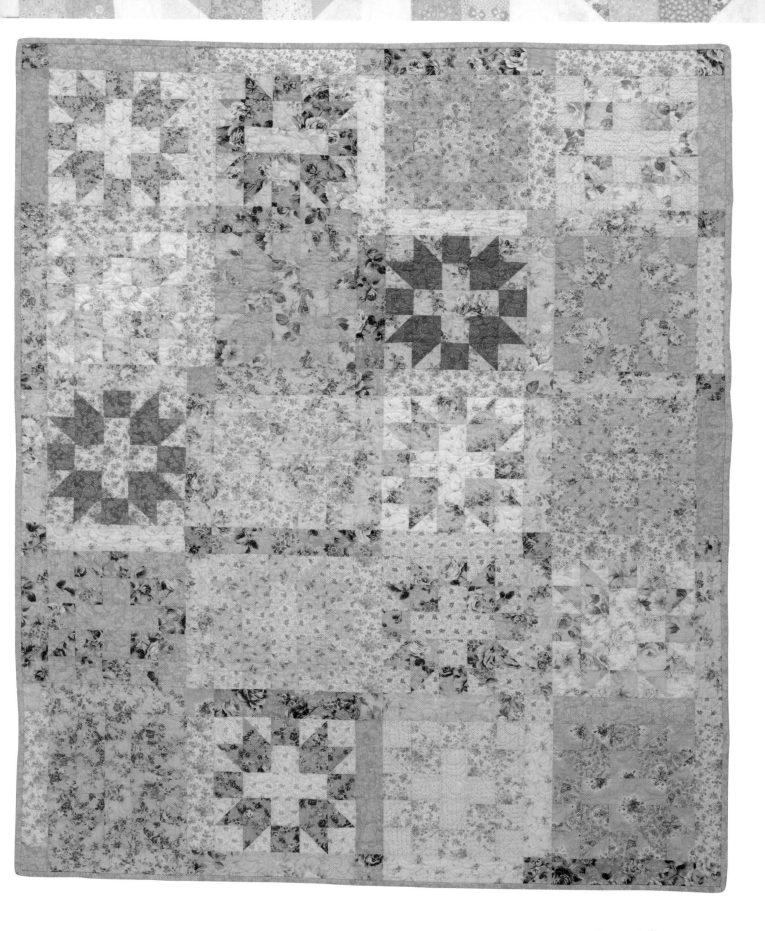

3. Making Unit 3: sew one half-square triangle unit to a Fabric A square, as shown below. Press towards the square.

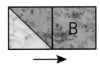

4. Sew one half-square triangle unit to a Fabric B square, as shown. Press towards the square.

5. Sew these units together, pinning the intersection to ensure a perfect match to form Unit 3. Make four of these units. Press the seam as shown.

Unit 3

6. Rotate one Unit 3 and sew to either side of Unit 1, pinning at the seam intersections to ensure a perfect match. Make two of these units. Press as shown.

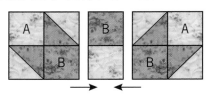

7. Rotate one of these units and sew it to either side of Unit 2. You have now made one block.

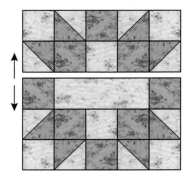

8. Repeat with your other piles to make twenty blocks in total.

Assembling the Quilt Top

- Lay out your blocks, four across and five down, with the sashing strips in between as shown below.
- Choose thirty of the 2½in squares you have set aside for sashing squares and lay these between the sashing strips. The remaining ten can be kept for a future project.
- Make sure you are happy with the placing of each block, sashing strip and sashing square before sewing.

- Sew the sashing squares to the sashing strips as shown and sew to the block. Join four blocks to form each row.
- The top row and the next three rows will have the sashing joined as shown.
- The bottom row will have the sashing joined as shown.
- Sew the rows together (see diagram, right). Pin at every seam intersection to ensure perfect alignment.
- Your quilt top is complete. Quilt as desired and bind to finish (page 124).

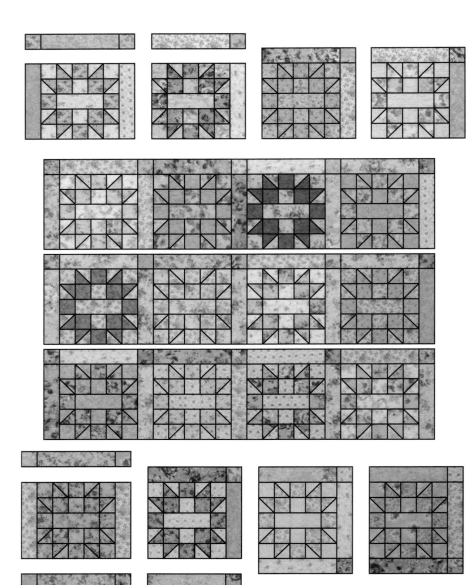

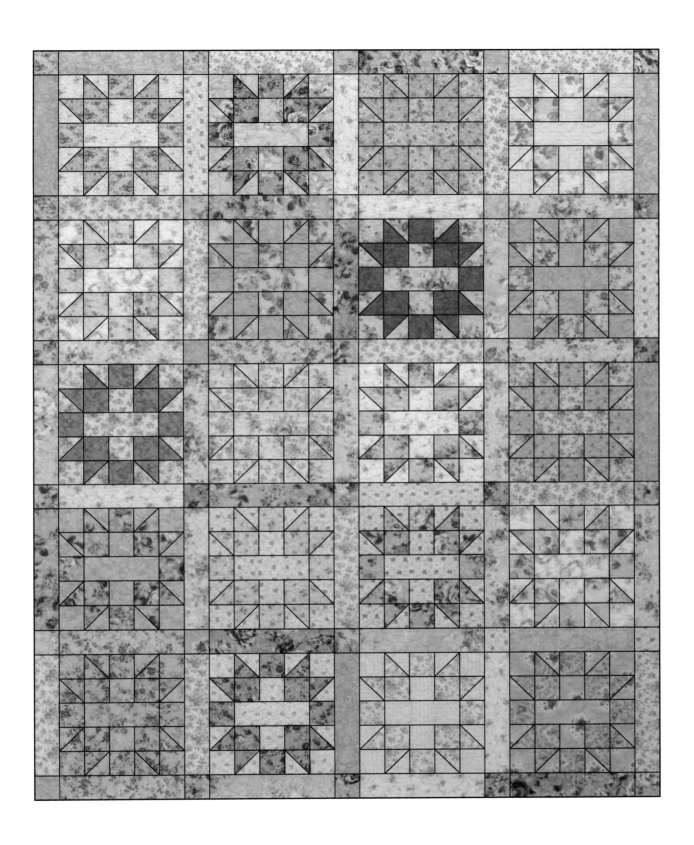

Jitterbug

Vital statistics

Quilt size:	56in x 72in
Block Size:	12in
Number of blocks:	12
Setting:	3 x 4 blocks
	with 4in sashing
	plus 2in plain border
	and 4in stripe border

What a bright and cheerful design this is! The liberal use of white really makes all the colours sing. The combination of different units – four-patch units, flying geese units and half-square triangles – makes for a bold and interesting block and when these are combined with eyecatching sashing and a striped border it makes up into a dynamic quilt. We have used reproduction Thirties fabrics mixed with a really fresh white on white.

What you need

- One jelly roll **or** forty 2½in strips cut across the width of the fabric
- 102in (260cm) background fabric
- 20in (50cm) fabric for binding
- Omnigrid 96 triangular ruler (or similar)

opposite:
This bold, graphic design is given a softer overall appearance by using charming reproduction Thirties fabrics, freshened with a white background fabric. The quilt was pieced by the authors and longarm quilted by The Quilt Room.

Cutting Instructions

Jelly roll:

- Take six strips and cut each into eight 2½in x 4½in rectangles. You need to make a total of forty-eight.
- Take twelve strips and cut each into three 2½in x 12½in rectangles. You need to make a total of thirty-four.
- Leave twenty-two strips uncut – eight of these will be used for making the half-square triangles, six will be used for the four-patch blocks and eight will be used in the stripe border.

Background fabric:

- Cut thirty-nine 2½in strips across the width of the fabric. Set six aside for the plain border.
- Sub-cut six strips into 2½in x 4½in rectangles. You need forty-eight.
- Sub-cut eleven strips into 2½ in x 2½in squares. You need 164.
- Leave sixteen strips uncut – eight will be used for making the half-square triangles and eight will be used in the stripe border.

Binding:

- Cut into six 2½in wide strips across the width of the fabric.

Seam allowance:

- Use scant ¼in seams throughout.

tip

This quilt requires the use of the Omnigrid 96 triangular ruler to make 2in half-square triangles from a 2½in wide strip. If you are using another speciality triangle, please ensure you are using the correct markings.

Making the Half-Square Triangle Units

1. Take the eight Thirties strips and eight background strips allocated for the half-square triangle units.

2. Press one Thirties strip and one background strip right sides together ensuring that they are exactly one on top of the other. The pressing will help hold the two strips together (see the diagram below).

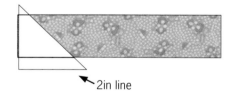

3. Lay out on the cutting mat and trim the selvedge on the left side. Position the ruler as shown below, lining up the 2in mark at the bottom edge of the strips, and cut the first triangle. The cut out triangle has a flat top – this would have been a dog ear that you needed to cut off, so you are saving time!

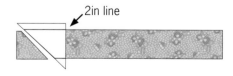

2in line

4. Rotate the ruler 180 degrees to the right (see below) and cut the next triangle. Continue along the strip. You need twenty-four sets of triangles from one strip.

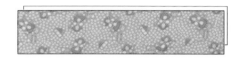

2in line

5. Sew along the diagonals to form twenty-four half-square triangles (see below). Trim the dog ears and press open with the seams pressed towards the Thirties fabric.

6. Repeat with the other seven Thirties and background strips. You need 192 half-square triangles in total.

7. You should now have eight different half-square triangle units. Divide them into two sets of four units and label them Set 1 and Set 2 (see below).

Set 1   Set 2

8. Working with Set 1, take two half-square triangles and sew together as shown below. Press in one direction. Sew the other pair together and press in the other direction.

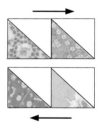

9. Sew the two pairs together, pinning the centre seam to ensure a perfect match, to form unit A. Press as shown below. Make twenty-four of these Unit As. Repeat with Set 2 to make another twenty-four Unit As.

Unit A

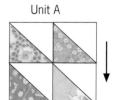

Making the Flying Geese Units

1. Take one background 2½in square and lay it right sides together on a 2½in x 4½in Thirties rectangle. Sew across the diagonal as shown below.

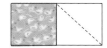

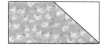

tip

When sewing across the diagonal in step 1 above, you may like to draw the line in first to mark your stitching line, but after sewing a few, you will probably find further marking is unnecessary.

2. Flip the square over and press towards the background fabric (see diagram below). Trim the excess background fabric but do not trim the Thirties fabric. Although this creates a little more bulk, this Thirties rectangle keeps your flying geese in shape.

3. Place a second background 2½in square and lay it on the other side as shown in the diagram below and sew across the diagonal.

4. Flip the square over and press. Trim excess background fabric (see below). Repeat to make forty-eight units.

5. Sew a 2½in x 4½in background rectangle to a flying geese unit, as shown below, to form Unit B. Press towards the background rectangle. Make forty-eight of unit B.

Unit B

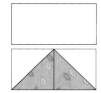

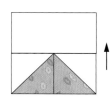

tip

Don't stackpile your strips when cutting the segments for the four-patch blocks. Check you are cutting perfect rectangles by putting one of your ruler guides on the seam line.

Making the Four-Patch Units

1. Take two of the four-patch strips and, with right sides together, sew down the long side. Open and press to the darker side (see diagram below). Repeat with the other four strips allocated for the four-patch blocks.

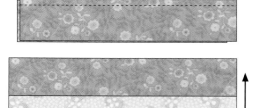

2. Trim the selvedge and cut 2½in segments from each strip unit (as shown in the diagram below). You need thirty-six in total.

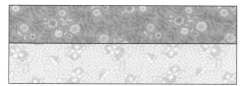

3. Rotate half of the segments and chain piece together to form eighteen four-patch blocks, pinning the centre seam to ensure a perfect match.

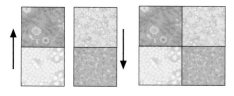

Assembling the Blocks

1. Sew a Unit B to either side of a centre four-patch unit. Press towards the four-patch. Make twelve of these centre rows.

Unit B   Unit B

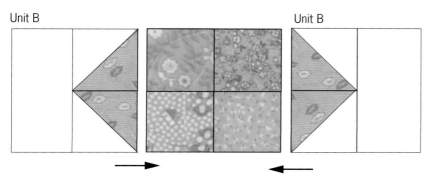

2. Sew a Unit A from Set 1 and a Unit A from Set 2 to either side of a Unit B. Press towards Unit B. Make twenty-four of these rows.

Unit A (Set 1)   Unit A (Set 2)

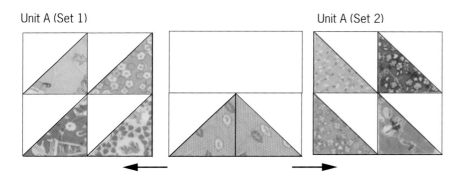

3. Rotate half of these rows and sew to either side of the centre row, pinning at seam intersections to ensure a perfect match.

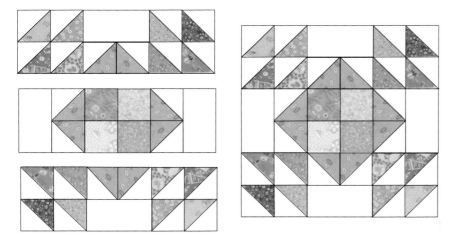

tip

You can make your blocks as scrappy as you like but we chose to have the same colour flying geese in each block.

Sewing the Sashing Strips

1. Take a background 2½in square and lay it right sides together on one end of a 2½in x 12½in Thirties rectangle and sew across the diagonal, as shown below.

2. Flip the square over and press towards the background fabric.

3. Trim the excess background fabric but do not trim the Thirties fabric, as this maintains the shape. Sew another background 2½in square on the other end and sew as before. Press and trim. Make thirty-four of these sashing strips.

4. Sew into pairs to create seventeen sashing units, pinning at triangle points to create a perfect match.

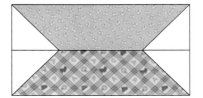

Assembling your Quilt

1. Row A: sew three blocks and two sashing units together to form Row A. Press seams in the direction shown by the arrows in the diagrams below. Make four of these rows.

Row A

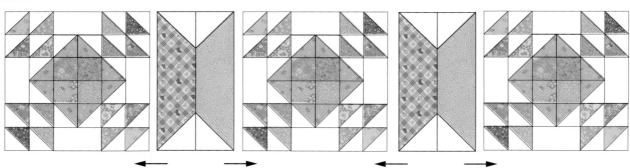

2. Row B: sew three sashing units and two four-patch blocks together to form Row B. Press seams as shown. Make three of these rows.

Row B

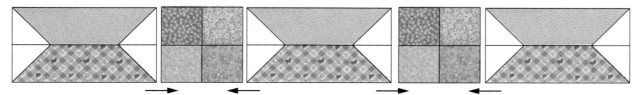

3. Referring to the diagram below, sew the rows together. Your seams should nest together nicely. Pin at every seam intersection to ensure perfect alignment.

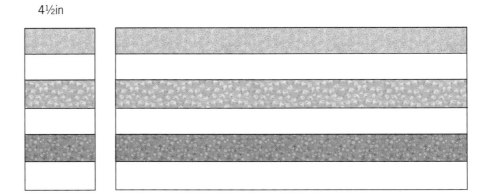

Piecing the Striped Border

1. Sew three Thirties strips alternating with three background strips. Press seams to Thirties fabric, as shown right. To prevent the strip unit 'bowing', press after each strip is added. Trim the selvedge and sub-cut into nine 4½in segments. Repeat with another three Thirties and three background strips.

2. Cut the remaining two Thirties strips and two background strips in half and join three Thirties half strips and three background half strips. Sub-cut into four 4½in segments. You need twenty in total, so you'll have two spare.

3. Sew two lengths of four segments together for the top and bottom borders and two lengths of six segments for the side borders (see diagram below).

4½in

tip

Dull or bent needles can snag and distort your fabric and cause your machine to skip stitches, so be sure to change needles frequently.

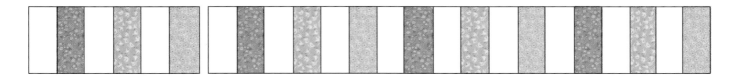

Adding your Borders

- Join your plain border strips together to form a long length. Determine the horizontal measurement from side to side through the centre of your quilt top. Cut two lengths of border strips to this measurement and sew one to the top and one to the bottom of the quilt, pinning and easing wherever necessary.

- Determine the vertical measurement from top to bottom of the quilt top. Cut two lengths to this measurement and sew to either side of the quilt, pinning and easing where necessary.
- Sew and pin the top and bottom stripe border in place and press. Now sew on the side borders, pinning and easing where necessary. Press the work.
- Your quilt top is now complete. Quilt as desired and bind to finish (see page 124).

Hexagon Hip Hop

Vital statistics

Quilt size:	56in x 62in
Half Hexagons per row:	8
Number of Rows:	10

There's nothing subtle about the range of fabrics in this quilt! They are from American Jane's Recess range from Moda. The hexagons are not true hexagons in the exact sense of the word but they certainly give the appearance of hexagons. They are actually half hexagons sewn into vertical rows and this makes the design much easier to machine piece. The only thing that you have to keep an eye on is the placement of the fabrics to create the hexagons but once you have got the idea, this quilt goes together very quickly. The offcuts from the layer cake are used to create the border, which finishes the quilt off nicely and means that there is no wastage.

If you prefer subtle, the variation quilt shown on page 71 will be just your cup of tea as it uses a range of Japanese taupes from Daiwabo.

What you need

- One layer cake **or** forty 10in squares
- 28in (70cm) border fabric
- 20in (50cm) binding fabric
- Quilting ruler with 60 degree angle

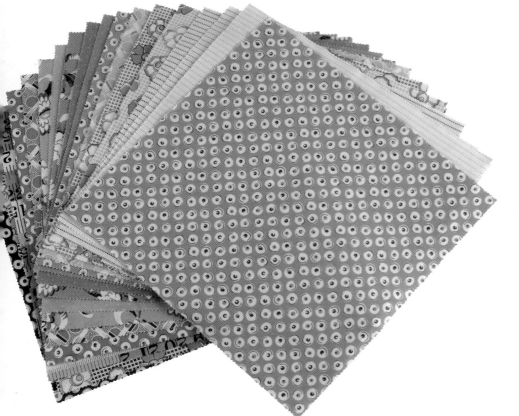

opposite:
Hexagon Hip Hop uses fabrics with the 'wow!' factor from Recess by American Jane. The visibly eye-catching bright 1940s retro fabrics couldn't fail to brighten up any room. We chose an orange toned variegated thread and a retro daisy quilting pattern to enhance the design – nothing subtle here! The quilt was pieced by the authors and longarm quilted by The Quilt Room.

Cutting Instructions

Layer cake squares:

- Cut a 10in square in half to make two rectangles 5in x 10in. Lay one rectangle exactly on top of the other, both right side up, and press to hold them in place.

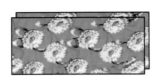

- Take a quilting ruler with the 60 degree angle marked and line up a marked 60 degree line along the bottom of the rectangle, ensuring that the corner of the ruler is on the bottom right-hand corner of the rectangle. Double check that your ruler is in the correct position before cutting and then cut along the edge of the ruler.

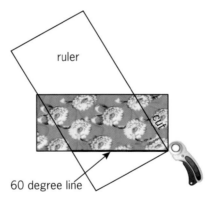

- Rotate the ruler and repeat on the other side and cut along the edge of the ruler. Double check your ruler is in the correct position before cutting.

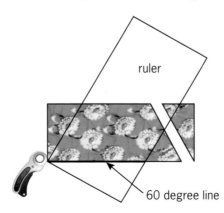

> **tip**
>
> If using a Creative Grids ruler, when your ruler is right side up facing you, you have to rotate it clockwise for the right-hand cut and anti-clockwise for the left-hand cut.

- Place these new units into three separate piles:
  Pile 1 – a pile of half hexagons, keeping the two from the same fabric together
  Pile 2 – a pile of triangles from the right-hand cut
  Pile 3 – a pile of triangles from the left-hand cut.

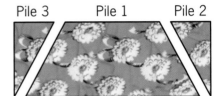

- Repeat this until all of your 10in squares have been cut into half hexagons and triangles.

> **tip**
>
> Once you feel confident with your technique, you can speed up the cutting of your hexagons by layering two or three squares together. However, do make sure you don't try to cut through too many as you will lose accuracy.

Assembling the Quilt

1. The half hexagons are sewn together in downward rows using scant ¼in seams and the hexagons are formed when two half hexagons of the same fabric are sewn together. You need to take care with the placement of the fabrics so it is best at this stage to lay out your half hexagons referring to the diagram below. You will soon get the hang of alternating a half hexagon, which has to match the one in the previous row, with a new hexagon, which will be matched up in the next row.

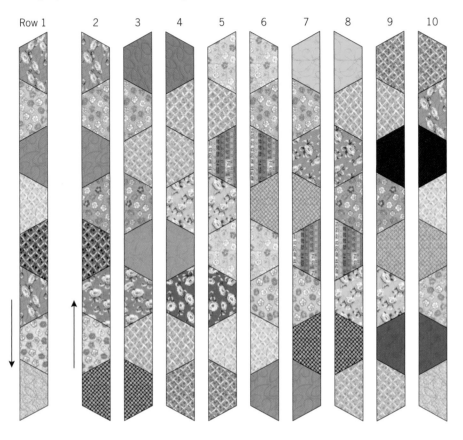

2. When you are happy with the layout, starting with Row 1, sew the half hexagons into vertical rows. Label the rows as you don't want to mix up your rows at a later stage. Note that when sewing the half hexagons together, because you have an angled cut, they will appear to be ¼in out at each end (see diagram below).

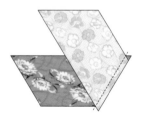

3. It is important to check that your edges are straight so check the alignment after you have sewn your first two half hexagons together.

4. Press Row 1 with the seams down, Row 2 with the seams up and continue to press the seams in alternate directions. This will ensure that when you sew the rows together all of the seams will nest together nicely.

5. Sew the rows together as shown in the diagram below, pinning at each intersection to ensure a perfect match.

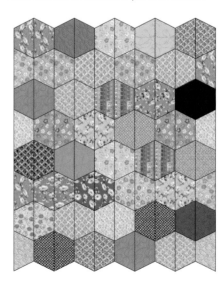

Sewing the Inner Border

1. Join six of the 2½in border strips together to form a long length. Determine the vertical measurement from top to bottom through the centre of your quilt top. Cut two side borders to this measurement. Pin and sew to the quilt, easing if necessary.

2. Determine the horizontal measurement from side to side across the centre of the quilt top. Cut two borders to this measurement. Pin and sew to the quilt.

3. Once these top and bottom borders have been sewn, the excess hexagon fabric can be trimmed. Press towards the border fabric.

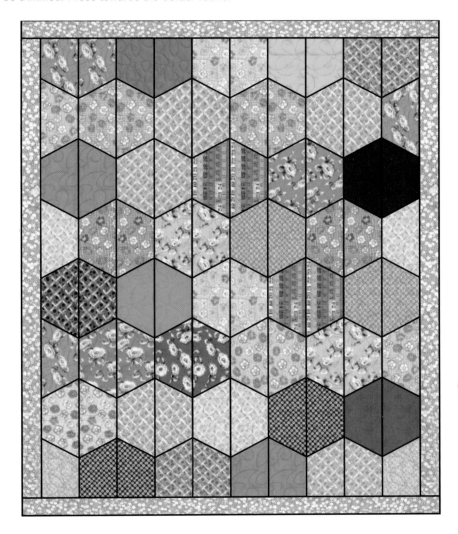

tip

Keep a stack of small scraps beside your sewing machine and always use one to finish a row of sewing, keeping it under the machine foot until you are ready to start sewing again. There is then no need to waste thread when starting to sew by holding on to the ends, as you are all ready to go. More importantly, you don't have to spend endless hours snipping thread ends off your quilt.

Sewing the Outer Border

1. Take two triangles from the right-hand cut and sew into a rectangle. Note that when you are sewing the triangles together they will overlap at each end, as shown in the diagram below. Trim the dog ears and press towards the darker fabric. Repeat with the rest of the triangles from the right-hand cut.

tip

When pressing it is better to press without steam, as steam can distort smaller pieces of fabric. Definitely do not use steam if there are any bias edges in your work.

2. Sew eighteen rectangles together and sew a 4½in x 7in rectangle to each end, and then press. Sew twenty-two rectangles together and sew a 4½in x 9in rectangle to each end and press. These borders will need to be trimmed once you have measured your quilt.

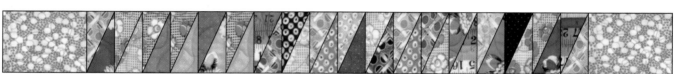

3. Repeat with the left-hand cut to create two more borders.

tip

When creating your border, if you mix your right-hand cuts with your left-hand cuts it creates a different effect – something to bear in mind for your next quilt!

4. Determine the horizontal measurement from side to side across the centre of the quilt top. Trim these two borders to this measurement, trimming some from each end so the border pattern is central. Pin and sew to the quilt, and then press.

5. Determine the vertical measurement from top to bottom through the centre of your quilt top. Trim the two side borders to this measurement. Pin and sew to the quilt and then press.

6. Your quilt top is now complete. Quilt as desired and bind to finish (see page 124).

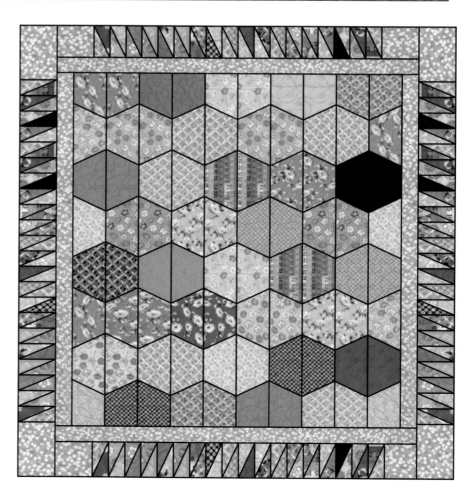

Our variation uses a range of Japanese taupes from Daiwabo – just to show that we can do 'subtle' too! The quilt was pieced by the authors and longarm quilted by The Quilt Room.

Stepping Stones

Vital statistics

Quilt size: 72in x 96in
Block size: 12in
Number of blocks: 48
Setting: 6 x 8 blocks

Jelly Roll Only Version
Size: 54in x 78in
Blocks per quilt: 24
Setting: 4 x 6 blocks
plus 3in border

This combination of jelly roll and layer cake makes a lovely big quilt. However, if you don't need such a large quilt, then you can opt for the jelly roll version, which has the central twenty-four blocks only. This clever quilt uses one jelly roll for the centre and one layer cake for the outside blocks. Having the outer border creates another dimension to the design but if you want a smaller quilt then the centre alone looks great – see the variation on page 79, which is just the centre using a black and white jelly roll, with red and grey for the additional fat quarters.

You will need to do a bit of sorting of colours but don't get too hung up about using a green instead of a blue or a brown or green with the reds. It is all part of the charm of scrap quilts – and isn't that why we love creating quilts from jelly rolls and layer cakes?

You do need to add some extra fat quarters and you can juggle these about if you feel you are short of a certain colour.

What you need

- One jelly roll and one layer cake
- Four fat quarters blue
- Four fat quarters red
- Four fat quarters light
- 26in (65cm) fabric for binding, cut into nine strips 2½in wide across the width of the fabric

Jelly Roll Version:
- One jelly roll
- Four fat quarters red
- Four fat quarters light
- 28in (70cm) border fabric, cut into seven 3½in strips
- 20in (50cm) for jelly roll version cut into seven 2½in wide strips)

opposite:
This quilt uses Portobello Market from Moda's Three Sisters – a lovely mix of red, blue, green and brown. One jelly roll was used for the centre of the quilt and a layer cake was chosen for the outer border to make a very large bedsize quilt. The quilt was pieced by the authors and longarm quilted by The Quilt Room in a traditional feather design.

Making the Four-Patch Blocks

1. Sort the jelly roll into nine light strips, nine blue strips and eighteen assorted red. Set the red strips aside for the moment.

2. Take the nine light and nine blue strips and cut them in half to form eighteen light strips of 2½in x 22in and eighteen blue strips of 2½in x 22in. Using a scant ¼in seam allowance, sew one light strip to one blue strip down the long side. Chain piece these for speed. Press towards the darker fabric.

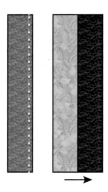

3. Layer two strip units right sides together, reversing the light and blue fabrics. Align the edges and make sure the centre seams are nesting up against each other. Sub-cut each into eight 2½in segments. Chain piece the segments together. Open out and press. You need seventy-two light and blue four-patch blocks. These are Unit A.

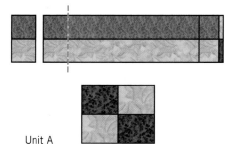

Unit A

4. Repeat the previous instructions with the eighteen red strips to form seventy-two assorted red four-patch blocks. You will have four spare from the jelly roll. Note: if you are only making the jelly roll version then you will only need forty-eight of these four-patch blocks and twenty-four can be saved for another project.

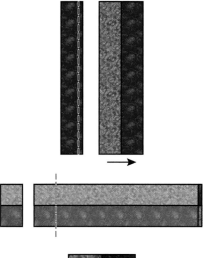

Unit B

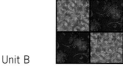

Cutting the Red and Light Fat Quarters

1. Take two red and two light fat quarters and layer them red fabric right side up and light fabric right side down. Press to hold them in place. Rotary cut into four 4⅞in strips and then sub-cut each strip into three 4⅞in squares (see diagram below).

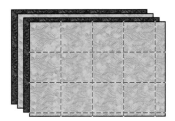

2. Cut across the diagonal of the squares to form triangles. These are now paired together, with a light triangle next to a dark triangle.

3. Without disturbing them too much, take them to the sewing machine and sew together along the diagonal, as shown.

4. Open and press to the darker fabric to form Unit C. Repeat with the other two red and two light fat quarters. You should get ninety-six Unit Cs from the fat quarters.

Unit C

---

tip

Don't be tempted to stackpile the strips when cutting segments for the four-patch blocks. If you want to speed things up and cut more than one strip unit at a time, lay the strip units butting up against each other on the cutting mat and cut through them with one cut. Always check you are cutting perfect rectangles by putting one of your ruler guides on the seam line.

Layer Cake Cutting Instructions

(Skip this section if you are only making the Jelly Roll version and go straight to 'Assembling Block Y'.)

1. Select twelve blue 10in squares and cut each into four squares 4½in x 4½in (see diagram below).

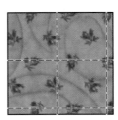

2. Take the four blue fat quarters and cut into 4½in strips and then sub-cut into 4½in squares You should get twelve from each fat quarter. You need a total of ninety-six blue 4½in squares.

Unit D

3. Divide the remaining twenty-eight 10in squares into reds (darks) and lights, bearing in mind that your reds can include anything that is not light!

4. Layer four of them together dark fabric right side up and light fabric right side down. Align the edges and press.

5. Rotary cut into four squares 4⅞in x 4⅞in and then rotary cut across the diagonal of the squares, as shown below. These are now paired together with a light triangle next to a dark triangle.

6. Without disturbing them too much, take them to the sewing machine and sew together along the diagonal as shown.

7. Trim dog ears. Open and press to darker fabric to form more Unit Cs.

8. Repeat with the remaining dark and light 10in squares. These will be added to your other Unit Cs. You need a total of 192.

9. Check that you now have four piles of units as follows:

Unit A – 72

Unit B – 72
(24 spare if making jelly roll quilt)

Unit C – 192
(96 if making jelly roll quilt)

Unit D – 96
(not needed if making jelly roll quilt)

Assembling Block Y

- If you are making the jelly roll version, then this is the only block you are going to make. Referring to the diagram below, sew your units into rows and your rows into blocks, pinning at every intersection to ensure a perfect match. Press as shown. You need twenty-four of Block Y.

tip

Before sewing each block, double check your placement of units. You must have the light squares in the blue and white four patches going diagonally across the block. You will lose the pattern if you get the half-square triangle units the wrong way round.

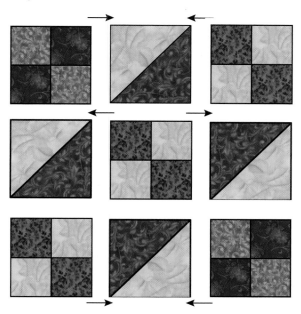

Assembling Block Z

- Referring to the diagram below, sew your units into rows and your rows into blocks, pinning at every intersection to ensure a perfect match. Press as shown. You need twenty-four of Block Z.

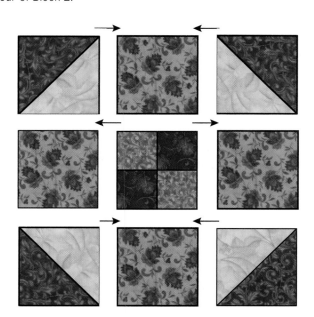

Assembling the Quilt

- Referring to the diagram below, lay out the blocks into rows. The top and bottom rows are comprised of only Block Z and the other rows will be Block Y with a Block Z at either end. Alternate the turning of Block Y so that the light diagonal squares go in opposite directions. If you are making the jelly roll quilt, then you will only have Block Ys.
- When you are happy with the layout, sew the blocks into rows and then sew the rows together. Pin at every seam intersection to ensure you have matching seams. Press.
- Your quilt top is now complete. If you are making the jelly roll version and wish to have a border, join your border strips into a continuous length and, referring to the general instructions on page 123, sew the border to your quilt top. Quilt as desired and bind to finish (see page 124).

Our variation shows just the central part of the quilt, which was made with just one jelly roll. We have used a black and white jelly roll and our additional fat quarters were shades of red and grey to add a touch of warmth. We have added a border in black to set off the design. This would be a great quilt to make for the man in your life! For the quilting we chose grey thread and used a swirl pattern so that the curves would complement the straight lines of the quilt. The quilt was pieced by the authors and longarm quilted by The Quilt Room.

Razzle Dazzle

Vital statistics

Quilt size:	52in x 52in
Block size:	8in
Number of blocks:	25
	plus 3in border
Setting:	blocks on point

This quilt is a combination of two similar blocks that look great when alternated. They are very simple to piece although look quite intricate. For added sparkle we have set them on point.

We chose a Moda range called Flag Day Farm from Minick & Simpson, which has a lovely range of blue, red and tan. It was very simple to sort the fabrics from this jelly roll. However, if you have a greater range of colours in your jelly roll you could put different colours in each block. It would create a different effect but that is what makes our quilts individual. Remember to keep an open mind as to the colour placement and be guided by what you have in your jelly roll.

Our variation on page 87 uses the gorgeous fabrics from Tanya Whelan of Grand Revival, which included many pinks and greens with highlights of grey, blue and red to create a soft pastel quilt with a hint of old-world vintage charm.

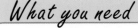

What you need

- One jelly roll **or**
  forty 2½in strips cut across
  the width of the fabric
- 24in (60cm) fabric for setting and
  corner triangles
- 20in (50cm) border fabric
- 20in (50cm) fabric for binding

opposite:
We have alternated two simple blocks and set them on point to create a complex-looking quilt, which is much easier to make than it looks – a good one to impress your family and friends! The quilt was pieced by the authors and longarm quilted by The Quilt Room in a small feather design.

Sorting your Strips

There will be two spare strips that can be saved for another project.

- **Block A:** (9 blocks)
  three light
  three red
  five tan
  three blue

- **Block B:** (16 blocks)
  four light
  four red
  eight tan
  eight blue

Cutting Instructions

Block A:
- Cut five tan strips into 2½in x 4½in rectangles. You get eight to a strip. You need thirty-six (four will be spare).
- Cut three blue strips into 2½in x 2½in squares. You get sixteen to a strip. You need thirty-six (twelve are spare).

Block B:
- Cut eight blue strips into 2½in x 4½in rectangles (eight to a strip). You need sixty-four.
- Cut eight tan strips into 2½in x 2½in squares (sixteen per strip, 128 in total).

Setting and corner triangles:
- Cut a 13in strip and sub-cut into three 13in squares. Cut across both diagonals of each of the squares to form twelve setting triangles.
- Cut a 7½in strip and cut into two 7½in squares. Cut across a diagonal of each square to form four corner triangles.

13in   7½in

Border fabric:
- Cut five 3in strips across the fabric width.

Binding fabric:
- Cut six 2½in strips across the fabric width.

Seam allowance:
- Use scant ¼in seams throughout.

Making Block A

1. Take one red strip and one light strip and, with right sides together, sew down the long side, as in the diagram below. Open and press to the red fabric.

2. Repeat with the other two light and red strips allocated for Block A.

3. Trim the selvedge and cut twelve 2½in segments from each strip unit. You need thirty-six in total.

4. Take a blue 2½in square and lay it right sides together on one end of a 2½in x 4½in tan rectangle. Sew across the diagonal as shown below. You may like to draw the diagonal line in first to mark your stitching line but after sewing a few, you may find it unnecessary. Flip the square over and press towards the blue fabric.

5. Trim the excess blue fabric but do not trim the tan fabric. Make thirty-six. Although not cutting the tan fabric creates a little more bulk, it does help to keep your units in shape.

6. Sew a red/light unit to a tan/blue unit as shown in the diagram below. Press. Make four of these to form one Block A.

7. Sew them together as shown and then press. You need nine Block As.

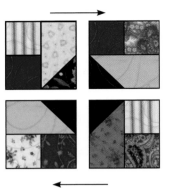

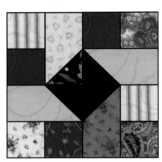

Block A

Making Block B

1. Take one red strip and one light strip and, with right sides together, sew down the long side. Open and then press to the red fabric.

2. Repeat with the other three light and red strips allocated for Block B.

3. Trim the selvedge and cut sixteen 2½in segments from each strip unit You need sixty-four in total.

4. Take a tan 2½in square and lay it right sides together on one end of a 2½in x 4½in blue rectangle. Sew across the diagonal as shown in the diagram below. You may like to draw the diagonal line in first to mark your stitching line but after sewing a few, you will probably find it unnecessary. Flip the square over and press towards the tan fabric.

5. Trim the excess tan fabric but do not trim the blue fabric. Although not cutting the blue fabric creates a little more bulk, it does help to keep your units in shape.

6. Take another tan 2½in square and lay it right sides together on the other end of the blue rectangle and sew across the diagonal as shown below. Flip the square over, trim and press towards the tan fabric. Make sixty-four.

7. Sew a red/light unit to a blue/tan unit as shown below. Press. Make four of these to form one Block B.

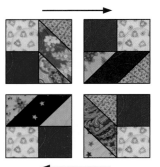

8. Sew them together as shown in the diagram below and press. You need sixteen Block Bs. As in Block A they can be as scrappy as you like.

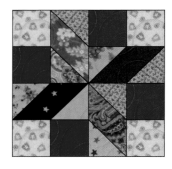

Block B

Setting Blocks On Point

- Referring to the diagram below, sew a setting triangle to each side of a Block B to create Row 1, making sure you align the bottom edges.
- Following the diagram, continue to sew the blocks together to form rows with a setting triangle at each end, pinning at every intersection to ensure a perfect match.
- Sew the rows together pinning at every intersection and sew the corner triangles on last. Trim edges, if necessary, to square up the quilt.

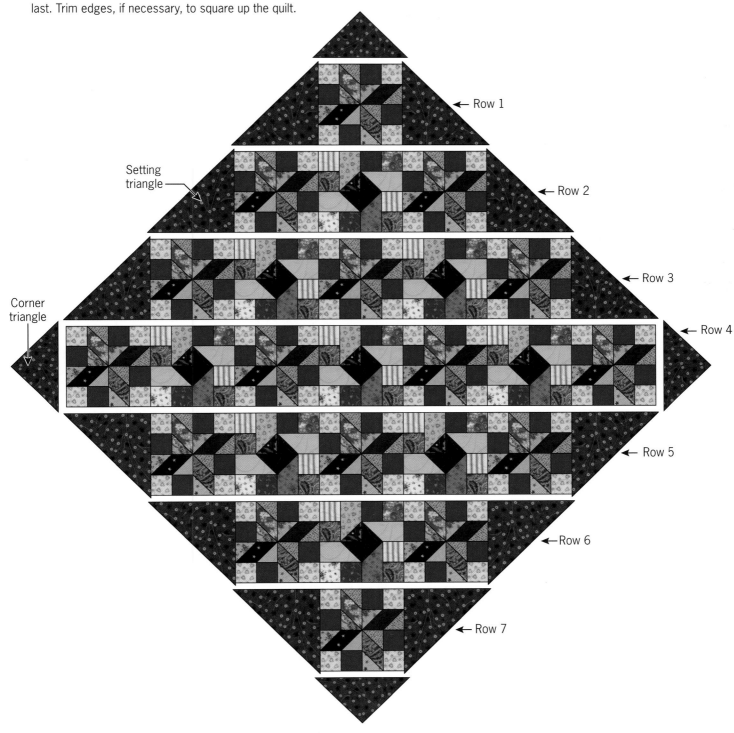

Finishing the Quilt

- Join your five 3in wide border strips into one continuous length and, referring to the instructions on page 123, add the borders to your quilt.
- Your quilt top is now complete. Quilt as desired and bind to finish (see page 124).

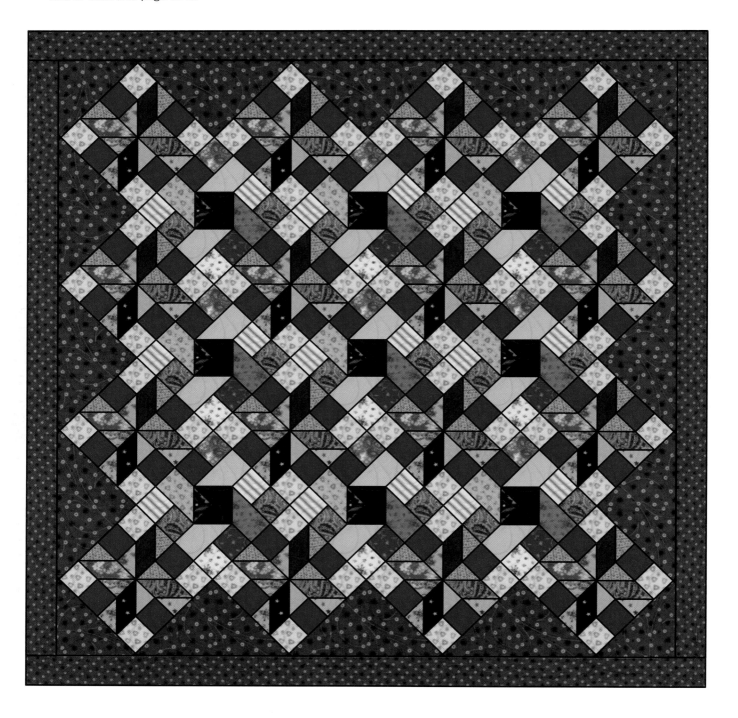

*Our variation uses the gorgeous fabrics from Tanya Whelan of Grand Revival, which include many pinks
and greens with highlights of grey, blue and red, creating a soft pastel quilt with a hint of old world charm.
The quilt was pieced by the authors and longarm quilted by The Quilt Room.*

Twisting the Night Away

Vital statistics

Quilt size:	62in x 74in
Block size:	9½in
Number of blocks:	32 plus
	3½in border
Setting:	on point

This is an effective combination of two blocks. One is a snowball block and the other is a twist block, easily sewn by partially sewing the first seam. Setting it on point completes the effect.

Our version using Kaffe Fassett fabrics shows the twist block quite plainly but we decided to be rather more subtle with our variation, shown on page 93, and allow the distinctive Heather Bailey fabrics to dictate the design and the twist to blend in rather than stand out. It just shows how different you can make a quilt look just by changing the focus. This is a great quilt for using large, bold floral prints.

What you need

- One layer cake **or** forty 10in squares
- 24in (60cm) dark twist fabric
- 24in (60cm) light twist fabric
- 1¼yd (1.1m) for setting triangles (this could be the same fabric as one of the twist fabrics)
- 24in (60cm) fabric for binding

opposite:
Twisting the Night Away uses the distinct fabrics from Kaffe Fasset and for the twisted ribbons we used a light and a dark mauve which showed the twists in the ribbons quite distinctly. The quilt was pieced by the authors and longarm quilted by The Quilt Room using a variegated thread to pick up all the colours in the fabrics.

Cutting Instructions

Layer cake:
- Choose twenty layers that you will leave as 10in squares.
- Choose a further twelve layers and cut a 6in strip from each.
- Sub-cut these into twelve 6in squares. Save the excess 4in x 10in rectangles and 4in x 6in rectangles for the border.
- Take the remaining eight layers and cut two 4in x 10in rectangles from each. Save these for the borders.

Dark twist fabric:
- Cut eight strips 2½in wide across the width of the fabric.
- Sub-cut six strips into 2½in x 8in rectangles. You get four to a strip. You need twenty-four.
- Sub-cut two strips into 2½in squares for the snowball corners. You get sixteen to a strip. You need thirty-one.

Light twist fabric:
- Cut eight strips 2½in wide across the width of the fabric.
- Sub-cut six strips into 2½in x 8in rectangles. You get four to a strip. You need twenty-four.
- Sub-cut two strips into 2½in squares for the snowball corners. You get sixteen to a strip. You need thirty-one.

Seam allowance:
- Use scant ¼in seams throughout.

Setting triangles:
- Cut two 14¾in wide strips across the width of the fabric and sub-cut into four 14¾in squares.
- Cut across both diagonals to form sixteen setting triangles (see diagram below). Two are spare.

- Cut one 8in wide strip across the width of the fabric and sub-cut into two 8in wide squares. Cut across one diagonal of these squares to form four corner triangles (see diagram below). Cutting the setting and corner triangles this way ensures the outer edges of your quilt are not on the bias.

Binding:
- Cut eight 2½in wide strips across the width of the fabric.

Making the Twist Blocks

1. Take one dark twist rectangle and, with right sides together, sew it only halfway down one side of a 6in square (see diagram below). Press open.

2. With right sides together, sew a light rectangle to the top of the square and press open.

3. With right sides together, sew a dark rectangle to the left side of the square and press open.

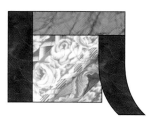

4. With right sides together sew a light rectangle to the bottom of the square and press open.

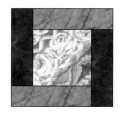

5. Now sew the first incomplete seam to complete the block. Repeat this process to make twelve twist blocks.

Making the Snowball Blocks

1. Draw a diagonal line from corner to corner on the wrong side of a dark 2½in square snowball corner.

2. With right sides together, lay the marked dark square on one corner of a 10in layer square, aligning the outer edges. Sew across the diagonal, using the marked diagonal line as the stitching line (see diagram below). After a while you may find you do not need to draw the line as it is not difficult to judge the sewing line. Alternatively, make a crease to follow.

3. Open the square out and press towards the outside of the block aligning the raw edges. Fold the corner back down and trim the excess snowball corner fabric

but do not trim the layer square (see first diagram below). Although this creates a little more bulk, keeping the layer square uncut will keep your unit in shape. Repeat on the other corner, as shown in the second diagram.

4. The snowball blocks have two, three or four snowball corners in both light and dark to create the pattern – see the six-part diagram below for the number of each you need to make.

Setting the Blocks on Point

1. Referring to the diagram below, sew a setting triangle to each side of a snowball block with two light corners to create Row 1.

2. Create Row 2 by sewing a snowball block with three dark corners to either side of a twist block with a setting triangle at each end.

3. Continue to sew the blocks together as shown to form rows with a setting triangle at each end. Sew the corner triangles on last.

4. Press towards the snowball block and your seams will nest together nicely.

Adding the Borders

- Join together the rectangles you set aside for the border to form a long length. You need a length of about 280in, so you will have a few spare. Follow the instructions on page 123 for sewing on the borders.
- Your quilt top is now complete. Quilt as desired and bind to finish (see page 124).

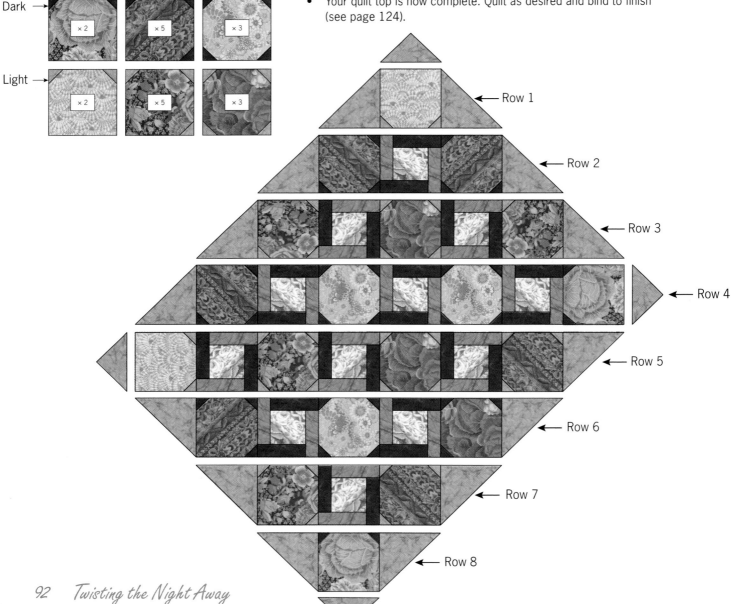

Our variation uses the bright and bold fabrics from Heather Bailey's Pop Garden range. We decided to use much more subtle colouring for the ribbons so that her stunning fabrics would stand out. We chose a plain aqua and an aqua dot, which certainly gives a quite different effect. The quilt was pieced by the authors and longarm quilted by The Quilt Room.

Stormy Weather

Blue and white has always been a favourite of ours and this design, which has only straight lines to sew, gives the appearance of curves. After making the quilt we thought how important it was to keep the star points dark so bear this in mind when sorting your jelly roll strips. You want to keep the circular movement that the design creates.

There's really no wastage with this quilt – you should know by now how we love to get the most from our jelly rolls! However, you could always treat yourself to an extra fat quarter if you find it difficult to be so frugal.

The variation on page 101 shows that the design works beautifully with a multicoloured palette too.

What you need

- One jelly roll **or** forty 2½in strips cut across the width of the fabric
- 3yd (2.65m) background and border fabric
- 20in (50cm) fabric for binding
- Omnigrid 96 triangular ruler (or similar)

opposite:
Stormy Weather is made from a blue jelly roll combined with white on white fabric to give a crisp, fresh look. You are only sewing straight lines but the design gives the appearance of curves creating a stunning circular movement. We chose a fun quilting design of sailing boats and used white thread to blend into the background. The quilt was pieced by the authors and longarm quilted by The Quilt Room.

Cutting Instructions

Background fabric:
- Cut seven 6½in strips across the width of the fabric and set aside for borders.
- Cut eleven 4½in strips across the width of the fabric and sub-cut each strip into nine 4½in squares. You need ninety-nine in total. Put seventeen aside to use in the sashing strips and eighty-two will have star points sewn to them.

Binding fabric:
- Cut seven 2½in strips across the width of the fabric.

Seam allowances:
- Use scant ¼in seams throughout.

Sorting your Jelly Roll Strips

- Choose three dark and three medium strips for the square in a square unit.
- Choose twelve assorted strips for the four-patch units. The remaining twenty-two strips will be used for making the star points.

Making the Four-Patch Units

1. Cut all twelve assorted strips in half to create twenty-four strips 2½in x 21in. Take two contrasting half strips and lay them right sides together. Sew down the long side as shown in the diagram below. Open and press to the darker fabric. Repeat the process and join the remaining assorted half strips into a total of twelve strip units, chain piecing for speed. Open and press to the darker fabric.

2. From each of your twelve strip units, sub-cut eight 2½in wide segments. You need a total of ninety-six segments.

3. Choose two segments and rotating one segment, sew together, matching the centre seams, as shown below. Your seams will nest together nicely. Make them as scrappy as you like. You need forty-eight four-patch units. Chain piece them for speed. Snip the thread between units and press open.

tip

For speed you can layer one strip unit right sides together with another, reversing light and dark. The seams will nest together nicely. When you sub-cut your 2½in wide segments, they will be ready to sew together to make your four-patch units.

Making the Square-in-a-Square Units

1. The square-in-a-square unit is made up of four half-square triangles, see below.

2. Press one dark and one medium strip right sides together, ensuring that they are exactly one on top of the other. Pressing in this way will help to hold the two strips together.

3. Lay out on a cutting mat and trim the selvedge on the left side. Position the Omnigrid 96 ruler as shown below, lining up the 2in mark at the bottom edge of the strips and cut the first triangle. You will notice that the cut out triangle has a flat top. This would just have been a dog ear you needed to cut off, so time is saved.

2in line →

4. Rotate the ruler 180 degrees to the right as shown below and cut the next triangle. Continue along the strip. You need to get twenty-four sets of triangles from one strip.

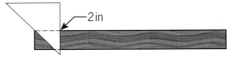
← 2in

5. Sew along the diagonals to form twenty-four half-square triangles. Trim all dog ears and press open. You would normally press towards the darker fabric but if you press half to the lighter fabric you will find the seams nest together nicely.

6. Sew into pairs and press all seams in the same direction. Rotate half and sew four together to form the square-in-a-square unit. Press. You now have six square-in-a-square units.

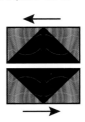

7. Repeat with the other two dark and two medium strips to make a further twelve units. You need eighteen in total. These can be as scrappy as you like but to create a more unified look, as we have done, use four of the same half-square triangles to make one unit.

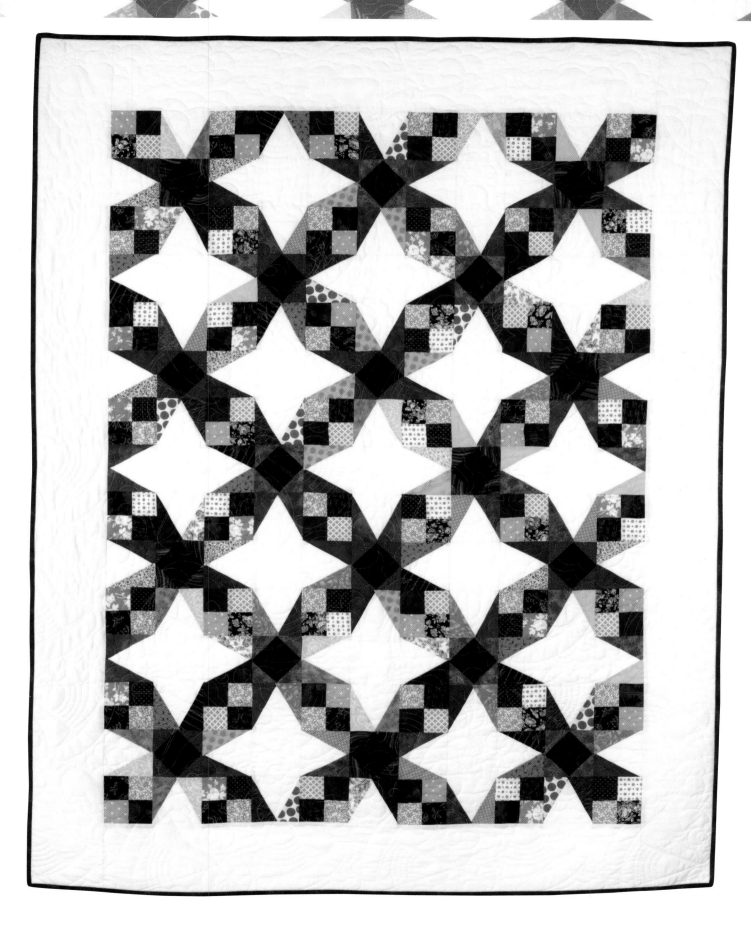

Making Star Point Units

1. Using the full size template provided on page 100, mark the sewing line on the wrong side of each of the eighty-two 4½in background squares. To do this, align the bottom of the template along the bottom of the background square and mark with a fine pencil line.

2. Place a marked background square, right sides together, over a jelly roll strip. Align your sewing line a scant ¼in in from the edge of the jelly roll strip. This is important as when flipped over there must be no background square showing. Sew along the marked line and continue to the edge of the square.

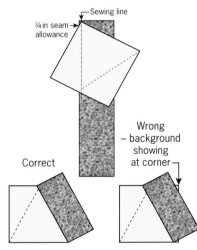

Correct

Wrong – background showing at corner

3. Test with one square before sewing lots, so you are confident that your seam allowance is correct. Once you are happy with your seam allowance, chain sew eight points per strip, leaving about ¼in between the squares. This is to enable you to sew eight squares per strip.

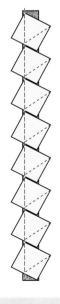

tip

When finishing sewing one square keep the needle point down in the fabric and lift the presser foot. Position the second square, leaving just enough space to cut between the squares.

4. Cut the squares apart and press. Trim the strip close to the square, although you do not need to square up at this stage.

5. Take another jelly roll strip and repeat to make the star points on the other side of the background square. Again, take care to ensure there is no background square showing when flipped over.

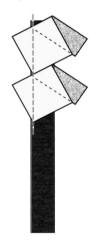

6. Cut the squares apart and press. Square up the units to measure 4½in. Repeat to make star points on eighty-two background squares.

tip

When squaring up the units, do so on the *reverse* of the fabric as you have your background square as a guide. Once you have squared up the unit to 4½in, you can then trim away the excess background fabric.

Assembling the Blocks

- Referring to the diagram below, lay out the units to form one block. You can make your blocks as scrappy as you like or more unified. Sew into rows and then sew the rows together to complete the block, pinning at every intersection to ensure a perfect match. Press as shown. Repeat to make twelve blocks.

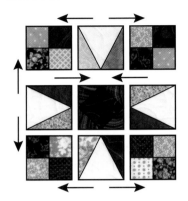

Assembling Sashing Strips

- Referring to the diagram below, sew a star point unit to either side of a plain background square. Press as shown. Repeat to make seventeen units.

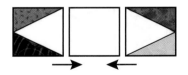

Assembling the Quilt

- Referring to the diagram below, create Row 1 by sewing three blocks together with a sashing strip in between. Pin at every intersection to ensure a perfect match. Press seams in the directions shown.
- Now create Row 2 by sewing three sashing strips together with a square-in-a-square unit in between. Pin at every intersection to ensure a perfect match. Press as shown.
- Sew the two rows together pinning at every intersection.
- Repeat Rows 1 and 2 twice more (to create Rows 3, 4, 5 and 6) and then finish with another row 1 (Row 7).

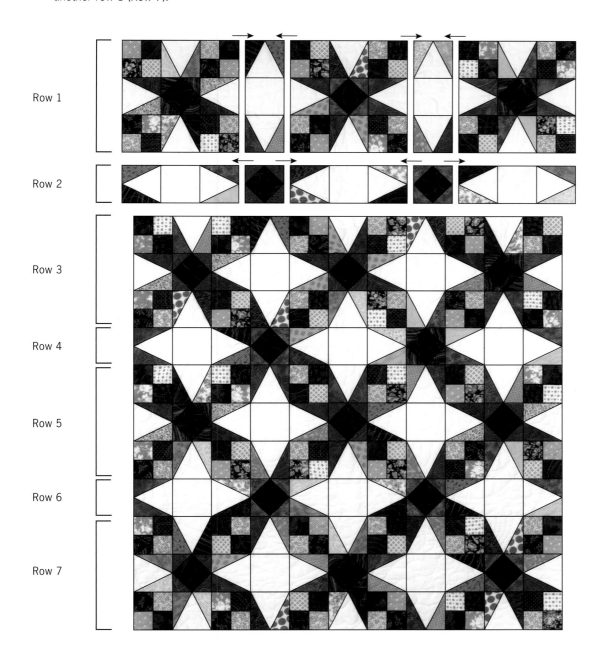

Finishing the Quilt

- Join your seven 2½in wide border strips into one continuous length and, referring to the instructions on page 123 and the diagram, right, add borders to the quilt.
- Your quilt top is now complete. Quilt as desired and bind to finish (see page 124).

tip

When storing a quilt, if you have room always roll it around a cardboard tube covered with acid-free paper. Alternatively, fold the quilt over acid-free paper and store in a pillowcase, which allows the fabric to breathe. It should be re-folded every few months, ensuring that the fold lines are made in different places. Never store quilts in plastic bags.

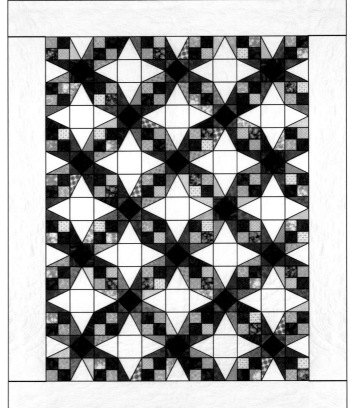

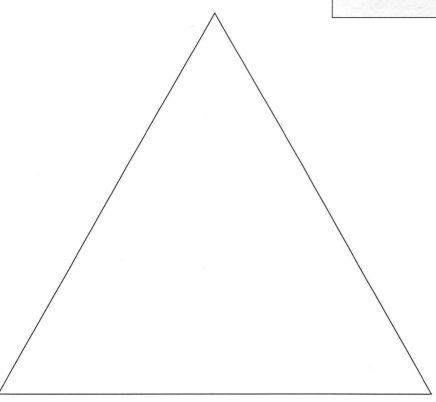

Trace this full-size template on to template plastic and cut out accurately.

In our variation we used Moda's Charisma by Chez Moi and, using such a multicolour jelly roll, we were prepared for a little work sorting the fabrics. No such thing – they just seemed to fall into place – and combined with a soft cream background created a really beautiful quilt. The quilt was pieced by the authors and longarm quilted by The Quilt Room.

Little Houses

Vital statistics

Quilt size:	58in x 58in
Block size:	9½in
Number of blocks:	25
Setting:	5 x 5 blocks plus 5in border

When thinking of how to use layer cakes, there is a tendency to think 'big'. This quilt however is totally the reverse and we definitely thought 'small'. Our little house blocks are only 4½in x 4½in so some of the pieces are quite tiny!

However, once your little house blocks are pieced, the layer cake squares are the perfect size for the frame, which tilts your houses in different directions. This quilt doesn't take as long as you think but some organization is needed.

You could of course have any 4½in block that you like in the centre knowing that your layer cake squares will frame them like this perfectly.

A selection of Japanese taupes was used for our quilt but just see how different you can make a quilt look when using different fabrics. Our variation on page 109 uses the clean, fresh colours from Grand Revival to create a completely different effect.

What you need

- One layer cake **or** forty 10in squares
- One fat quarter of light fabric for the background
- 1yd (1m) border fabric cut into six 5½in strips across the width of the fabric
- ½yd (0.5m) binding fabric cut into six 2½in strips across the width of the fabric

opposite:
Little Houses is made from a range of Japanese taupes by Daiwabo. We loved the earthy effect it gave the quilt. The quilt was pieced by the authors and longarm quilted by The Quilt Room.

Sorting your Layer Cake Squares

- You will need the following squares (you will have two spare).
  - five for house fabric
  - two for doors
  - one for windows
  - four for roof fabric
  - one for chimneys
  - twenty-five for frames.

Seam allowance:

- Use scant ¼in seams throughout.

House Construction

1. Cut six 1½in strips across a door square. Repeat with the other door square.

2. Cut six 1½in strips across a window square, as shown.

3. Cut six 1½in strips across one house square, see below.

4. Sew two house strips to two door strips and press. Sub-cut each into three 2½in segments, as shown below.

5. Sew one house strip to one window strip and press. Sub-cut into six 1½in segments.

6. Cut two house strips each into three 2½in segments. The remaining house strip from this square is spare.

7. Sew these units together to form the lower section of the house and press. You need to make six house sections with one house layer cake.

8. Repeat with the other house squares to make twenty-five house sections in total. You will have spare strips left over.

Roof Construction

1. Take the background fat quarter and, making sure you are cutting down the long side, cut the following pieces.

- For the roof construction (used below):
  - three strips 2in wide and sub-cut into twenty-five squares 2in x 2in.
  - two strips 1½in wide and sub-cut into twenty-five squares 1½in x 1½in.
- The following are to be set aside for the chimney units:
  - one strip 1¾in wide and sub-cut into two rectangles 1¾in x 10in.
  - two strips 2¾in wide and sub-cut into four rectangles 2¾in x 10in, and then trim one of these down to measure 1¾in x 10in.

2. Cut the roof squares into 4½in strips, as shown in the first diagram below. Sub-cut each strip into four segments 2in x 4½in, as shown in the second diagram. You need twenty-five in total.

3. Take a background 2in square and lay it right sides together on the right-hand side of a 2in x 4½in roof rectangle. Sew across the diagonal as shown below. You may like to draw the diagonal line in first to mark your stitching line or fold to mark a crease but after sewing a few, you will probably find it unnecessary. Flip the square over and press towards the background fabric.

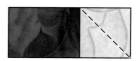

4. Trim the excess background fabric but do not trim the roof fabric. Lay a background 1½in square on the left-hand side and sew as before. Press and trim. Make twenty-five roof units.

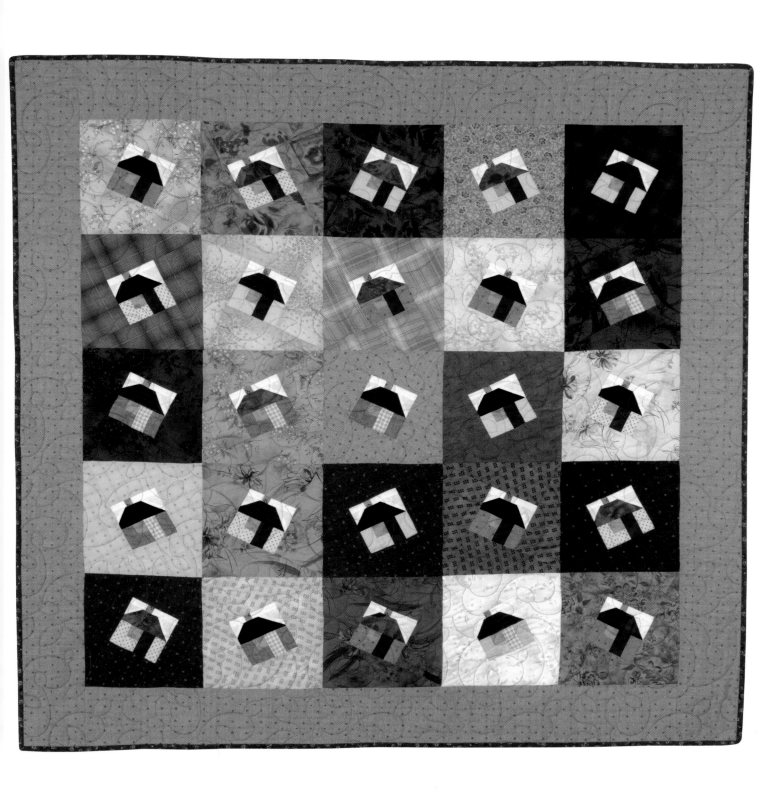

Chimney Construction

1. Cut three 1in strips from the chimney square, as shown below.

2. Sew a 1¾in x 10in background rectangle and a 2¾in x 10in background rectangle to either side of a chimney strip. Press and sub-cut into nine 1in segments.

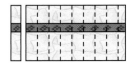

3. Repeat with the other two chimney strips. You need twenty-five chimney units.

4. Assemble your lower house section with the roof and chimney sections to form your house block. You need twenty-five blocks in total.

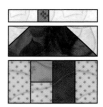

Framing your Blocks — Tilting to the Right

1. Take one layer cake square and right side up, cut it into two 5in strips. Cut each strip diagonally from bottom right to top left (see below). Notice that the right angle on your triangles is on the right-hand side – this is how you know that cutting in this direction will tilt your blocks to the right.

right angle on the right

2. Sew one triangle to a house block as shown below, lining up the corners and *only sewing halfway down* the triangle. Press the triangle open. Note that this is only partially seamed.

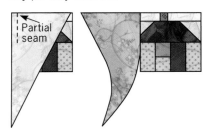
Partial seam

3. Sew a triangle across the top, lining up the corners as shown below. Press open. Don't worry about overlapping triangle points as you will trim the block later.

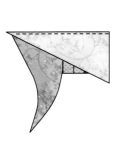
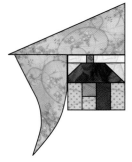

4. Sew the next two triangles in the same manner and then complete the first seam. Press the block open.

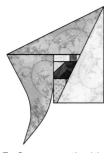
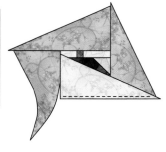

5. Square up the block to measure 10in square. Note: If your block is less than 10in, it won't matter as long as you square all the blocks to the same measurement. In total, you need to make thirteen blocks tilting to the right.

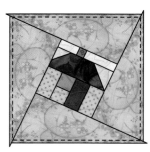

tip

Speed up the cutting by stacking the layer cake squares, aligning the edges and pressing to hold in place before cutting.

Tilting to the Left

1. To make the blocks tilt to the left, stack the layer cake squares and cut from the bottom left corner to the top-right corner. Notice that the right angle of the triangle is now on the left-hand side.

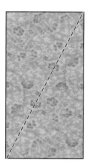 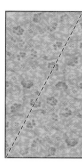 right angle on the left →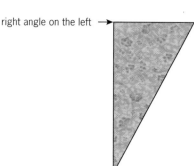

2. Sew the triangles to the block as you did in step 2 when tilting to the right, starting with a partial seam and always lining up the right-angled corner of the triangle with the corner of the house block. Press and square up your blocks. You need twelve blocks tilting to the left.

tip
Get into the habit of always snipping threads as you go. It will make a big difference to your work, keeping your patchwork neat and tidy.

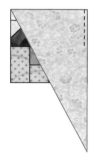 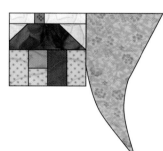 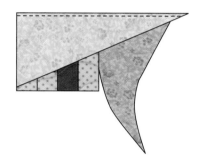

3. Referring to the diagram below, lay the blocks out and when you are happy with the layout sew the blocks into rows and then sew the rows together, pinning at every intersection to ensure a perfect match. Press the work.

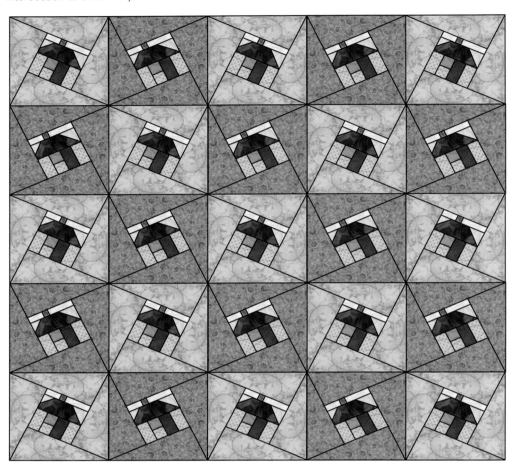

Sewing your Borders

- Join your border strips together to form a long length. Determine the vertical measurement from top to bottom through the centre of your quilt top. Cut the two side borders to this measurement (see diagram, right). Sew to the quilt.
- Determine the horizontal measurement from side to side across the centre of the quilt top. Trim these two borders to this measurement. Sew to the quilt.
- Your quilt top is now complete. Quilt as desired and bind to finish (see page 124).

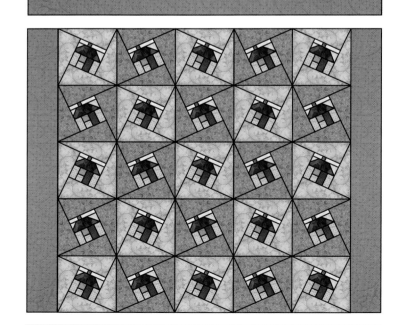

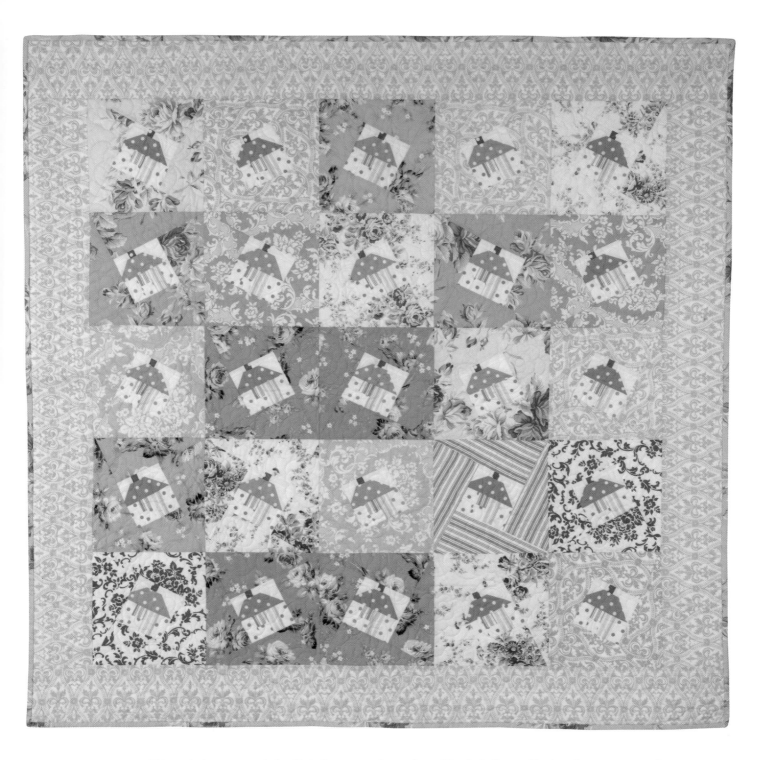

This variation was made by Chris Farrance who works at The Quilt Room. She loved our taupe version and offered to make the variation straight away. We decided on using the Grand Revival fabrics from Tanya Whelan and Chris cleverly chose the striped fabric for windows and doors.

Jelly Roll Hidden Wells

Vital statistics

Quilt size:	58in x 58in
Block size:	13in
Number of blocks:	16
Setting:	4 x 4 blocks plus 3in border

Back in 1989 Mary Ellen Hopkins, a lady well ahead of her time, created a wonderful pattern called Hidden Wells. With Mary Ellen's permission we have adapted the pattern to use with a jelly roll.

It does require a degree of concentration but it is well worth the extra effort. We hope you agree that the quilt design is stunning and looks amazingly complex. It certainly makes a beautiful quilt and would also look great as the centre for a medallion quilt surrounded by different borders. We used the Moda jelly roll called Louisa by Terry Clothier Thompson, which had a lovely mix of green, blue, tan and brown.

The pattern works best with different width strips so we cut one of our jelly roll strips in half lengthways to create two thin strips and added two other fabrics cut to different widths. Once you have made the quilt you will see the endless design possibilities.

Our variation on page 117 uses a pink and lilac range to create a very 'girly' first bed quilt. We just couldn't stop so we then made a large cushion from just one quarter of the quilt from the Hemming House range, choosing a purple spot for one of the accents, which added a great zing.

What you need

- One jelly roll **or** forty 2½in strips cut across the width of the fabric
- 20in (50cm) accent Colour 1 (cream)
- 20in (50cm) accent Colour 4 (red)
- 24in (60cm) border fabric
- Jelly roll strips for binding

opposite:
Thank you so much to Mary Ellen for allowing us to play with her great design. Once you've got to grips with the technique, you realize how many different effects you can make just by changing the width and number of strips in the strip unit – one technique, endless variations. The quilt was pieced by the authors and longarm quilted by The Quilt Room.

Sorting your Jelly Roll Strips

You need four colourways and eight strips in each. Our jelly roll fell beautifully into four distinctive colourways:
– green (Colour 2)
– blue (Colour 3)
– tan (Colour 5)
– brown (Colour 6).
Make sure there is a distinction between the colourways as you will lose the pattern if not. To create the best effect, the colours at the top need to differ from those at the bottom. Don't scatter a colour throughout, i.e., Strip 1 and Strip 7 should contrast. The remaining eight strips are for making the quilt binding.

Cutting Instructions

Accent colour 1 (cream):
- Cut eight strips 2in wide across the width of the fabric.

Accent colour 4 (red):
- Cut eight strips 1½in wide across the width of the fabric.

Colour 2 green jelly roll strips:
- Cut the eight green jelly roll strips in half along the length to make sixteen strips 1¼in x 42in.

Border fabric:
- Cut six strips 3½in wide across the width of the fabric.

Seam allowance:
- Use scant ¼in seams throughout.

tip
There are two main requirements when making this quilt – pressing and patience. Press each seam after sewing it and before adding another strip. If you wait until all your strips are joined together before pressing the units may not be straight and you will lose accuracy. As for patience, it is easy to get things mixed up so do not be in a hurry to lay out your blocks. Be patient and stay organized.

Making the Strip Units

1. Put your stacks of fabric in the correct order and label as follows:
Strip 1: Accent Colour 1 – cream 2in strip
Strip 2: Colour 2 – green 1¼in strip
Strip 3: Colour 3 – blue 2½in strip
Strip 4: Colour 2 – green 1¼in strip
Strip 5: Accent Colour 4 – red 1½in strip
Strip 6: Colour 5 – tan 2½in strip
Strip 7: Colour 6 – brown 2½in strip.

2. To make the first strip unit, select one strip from each stack. Referring to the diagram below, sew the strips together, pressing each seam before adding the next strip in order to prevent your strips from bowing. Press all seams in one direction, as indicated.

3. Repeat this procedure with your other strips to create eight strip units in total.

tip
You do need your strips to measure at least 42in. Discard any short strips as you will find you have insufficient fabric to cut four squares from the strip unit.

Making the Blocks

1. Take one strip unit and measure the width. It should measure 10½in. Trim the selvedge and cut four 10½in squares from the unit (see the diagram below). Don't panic if your measurement is slightly different – with so many seams to sew, it may well be! Cut your squares to that measurement but make sure *all* your squares throughout the quilt are cut the same size.

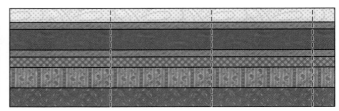

2. Using the four squares you have cut, cut each square across both diagonals and stack the triangles all in the same order. You will have four stacks and four triangles in each stack. Mark the stacks 1, 2, 3 and 4. We are going to be really organized!

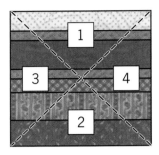 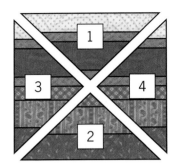

3. Take one Triangle 1 and pair it with Triangle 3 as shown in the diagram, right. Mark this Unit A. Repeat to make two of Unit A.

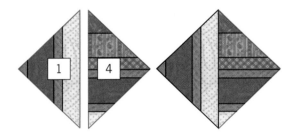

Unit A

4. Take one Triangle 1 and pair it with Triangle 4 as shown. Mark this Unit B. Repeat to make two of Unit B.

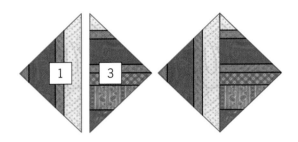

Unit B

5. Take one Triangle 2 and pair it with Triangle 3 as shown. Mark this Unit C. Repeat to make two of Unit C.

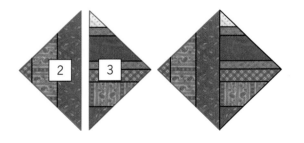

Unit C

6. Take one Triangle 2 and pair it with Triangle 4 as shown. Mark this Unit D. Repeat to make two of Unit D.
You should now have two each of Units A, B, C and D.

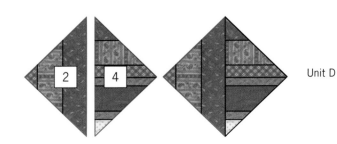

Unit D

7. Take the two Units A and D and sew together to form Block Y as shown below. Press towards Block A so the centre seams will nest together nicely.

8. Take the two Units B and C and sew together to form Block Z as shown. Press towards Block C so the centre seams will nest together nicely.

Block Y

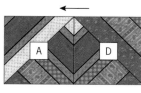

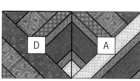

Block Z

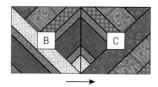

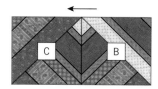

9. Sew Block Y to Block Z, press as shown below and relax for a moment!

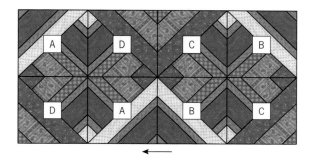

10. Repeat with another strip unit to form another Block Y and Block Z unit.

11. Rotate one of the Block Y and Z units and sew to the other to form one quarter of the quilt.

12. Repeat with the other jelly roll strips to complete the other three-quarters of your quilt. Join the quarters together and press.

tip

Bias edges will stretch if they are not handled carefully and this quilt has lots and lots of bias edges. Just remember to be gentle with no unnecessary handling and certainly no pressing with steam.

There is however an up side when working with bias edges and you will find this out when you start matching the seams. You will find that the bias edges will enable you to gently tweak the fabric into place and seams match up perfectly.

Sewing your Borders

- Join your border strips together to form a long length.
- Determine the vertical measurement from top to bottom through the centre of your quilt top. Trim the two side borders to this measurement. Sew to the quilt – see page 123 for further information.
- Determine the horizontal measurement from side to side across the centre of the quilt top. Trim these two borders to this measurement. Sew to the quilt.
- Your quilt top is now complete. Quilt as desired. Join your jelly roll strips and bind to finish (see page 124).

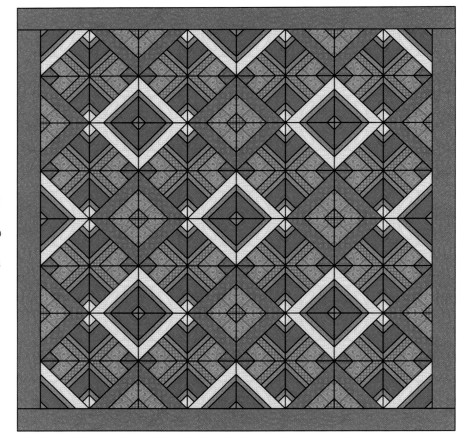

For our variation we used a pink and lilac jelly roll for this very girly quilt. The quilt was pieced by the authors and longarm quilted by The Quilt Room.

We loved making this design and got quite carried away. Our cushion, using Moda's Hemming House by Brannock & Patek is made from one quarter of the design and uses only eight jelly roll strips. This would be such a good project for using up any spare strips – just follow the instructions until you have made a quarter of the quilt! The cushion was pieced by the authors and longarm quilted by The Quilt Room.

English Country Garden

We try without fail to use every scrap of fabric from our jelly rolls, layer cakes and charm packs. There are instances, however, when you just can't help having something left over and it is handy to have a few projects, such as this pretty pillow, to use up these scraps.

Sometimes after all that speedy machine work it makes a nice change to sit back with a little hand sewing. English paper piecing is a relaxing way to use up your scraps of fabric. This method of patchwork can be used for any design but it is especially good for piecing intricate shapes such as hexagons. Refer to the paper piecing instructions on page 121 before starting this project.

What you need

- Thirty-five 5in neutral charm squares **or** background fabric 23in x 32in (58cm x 81cm)
- Sixteen 5in floral charm squares
- 1yd (1m) ric-rac ½in wide
- 1¼yd (1.25m) lace trim ½in wide
- Two fabric pieces 23in x 20in (58.5cm x 51cm) for the pillow backing

opposite:
A spare 5in charm square is perfect for the 2in size hexagon used in this cushion, and if you cut the 5in charm square into four 2½in squares that is just right for a 1in hexagon. Any jelly roll strip is also perfect for making 1in hexagons. Our project uses both and is intended to be a starting off point for you to create your own English Country Garden. Make it as abundant as you like and a bonus is that you won't ever have to get your hands dirty!

Cutting Instructions

- Take six of the floral charm squares and cut each into four 2½in squares. You need twenty-one.

Making the Cushion Front

1. If you are not starting with a 23in x 32in background fabric, create your background fabric by sewing the neutral charm squares into five rows of seven squares. Sew the rows together to form your background using scant ¼in seams throughout.

2. Refer to the basic instructions for English paper piecing opposite. Using the 5in floral charm squares and the 2in hexagon template, make seven 2in hexagons. Sew them together in a row.

3. Using the 2½in squares and the 1in hexagon template, make twenty-one 1in hexagons. Join seven together to form a flower rosette. Repeat this process to make two more flowers.

> **tip**
>
> When tacking the fabric squares over the hexagon paper template there is no need to cut the squares to size, although trimming a little from the corners makes it easier to sew.

4. Pin the 2in row of hexagons along the left of the background and hand stitch in place.

5. Place the three flowers on the background and pin in position. Insert the ends of the ric-rac under the flowers and hand stitch in place.

6. Stitch the ric-rac and lace embellishments in place.

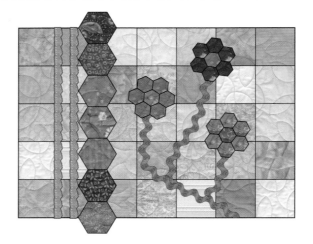

> **tip**
>
> Have fun in the creation of your own individual garden.

7. Quilt as desired and then make up the envelope pillow as follows:

- Hem a short end of each backing piece.
- With right sides together lay both backing pieces on to the pieced top and pin in place – they will overlap by about 4in (see diagram, right).
- Sew the seams using a generous ¼in seam allowance.
- Turn the pillow cover right sides out, insert a pad and your pillow is complete.

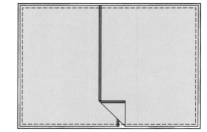

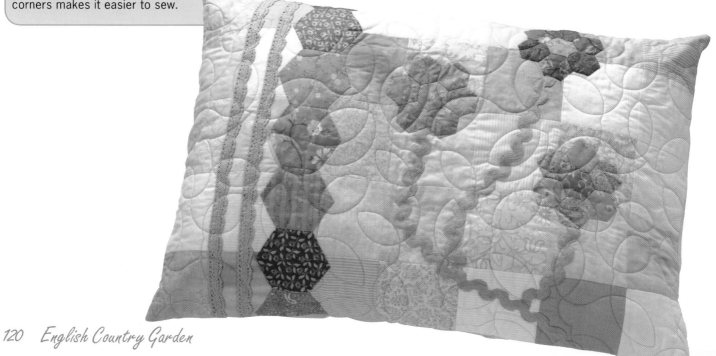

Basic instructions for English Paper Piecing

1. We have given templates below for 1in–2in hexagons going up in ¼in increments. Trace these on to plastic for a durable master template. You only need the 1in and 2in hexagons for this project, shown in red in the diagram below.

2. One paper template has to be made for every patch. These paper templates must be accurately cut and must be the exact size and shape of the finished patch. They can be re-used once the shapes are sewn together when the papers can be removed. Copying paper is a good weight. Draw around your master template with a fine marker and cut out accurately along the marked line.

tip

Keeping these paper templates accurate is the secret of success with this technique.

3. Place and pin the paper template to the wrong side of the fabric (see the diagram below). Cut fabric at least ¼in larger than the paper piece. This does not have to be absolutely accurate – it can be judged by eye.

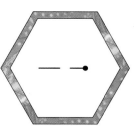

4. Fold the seam allowance over the paper and tack (baste) into position using big stitches and ensuring that corners are carefully folded. Sew right through the fabric and paper with a contrasting thread, so it can be seen easily for removal later.

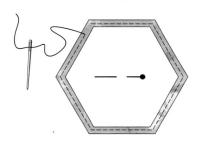

5. To join the patches, place right sides together and oversew together in a matching thread, just catching the edges of the fabric.

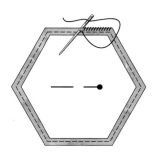

6. When all the pieces are sewn together in the shape required, press lightly and then remove the tacking (basting) thread and papers.

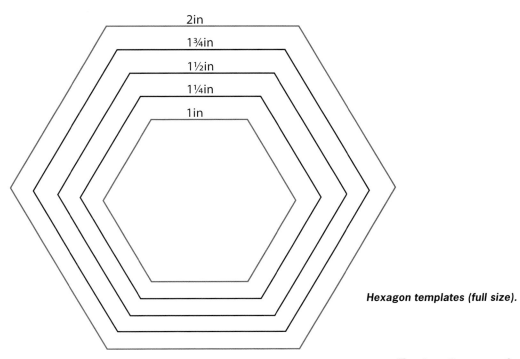

2in
1¾in
1½in
1¼in
1in

Hexagon templates (full size).

General Techniques

Tools

All the projects in this book require rotary cutting equipment. You will need a self-healing cutting mat at least 28in x 24in and a rotary cutter. We recommend the 45mm or the 60mm rotary cutter.

Any rotary cutting work requires rulers and most people have a make they prefer. We like the Creative Grids rulers as their markings are clear, they do not slip on the fabric and their Turn-a-Round facility is so useful when dealing with half-inch measurements. We recommend the 6½in x 24in as a basic ruler plus a large square no less than 12½in which is handy for squaring up and making sure you are always cutting at right angles.

We have tried not to use too many different speciality rulers but when working with 2½in strips you do have to rethink some cutting procedures. The Omnigrid 96 or the larger 96L is widely available from quilting suppliers. It is used for cutting half-square triangles as shown in Jitterbug, Damask Rose and Stormy Weather. If you are using any other tool, please make sure you are lining up your work on the correct markings.

Seams

We cannot stress enough the importance of maintaining an accurate ¼in seam allowance throughout. We prefer to say an accurate **scant** ¼in seam because there are two factors to take into consideration. Firstly, the thickness of thread and secondly when you press your seam allowance to one side, it takes up a tiny amount of fabric which has to be taken into consideration. These are both extremely small amounts but if they are ignored you will find your *exact* ¼in seam allowance is taking up more than ¼in.

It is well worth testing your seam allowance before starting on a quilt and most sewing machines have various needle positions that can be used to make any adjustments.

Seam Allowance Test

Take a 2½in strip and cut three segments 1½in wide (see diagram below). Sew two of the segments together down the longer side and press the seam to one side. Sew the third segment across the top. It should fit exactly. If it doesn't, you need to make an adjustment to your seam allowance. If it is too long, your seam allowance is too wide and can be corrected by moving the needle on your sewing machine to the right. If it is too small, your seam allowance is too narrow and this can be corrected by moving the needle to the left.

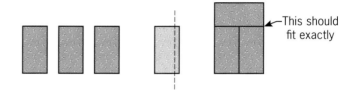
This should fit exactly

Pressing

In quiltmaking, pressing is of vital importance and if extra care is taken you will be well rewarded. This is especially true when dealing with strips. If your strips start bowing and stretching you will lose accuracy.

- Always set your seam after sewing by pressing the seam as sewn, without opening up your strips (see diagram below). This eases any tension and prevents the seam line from distorting.

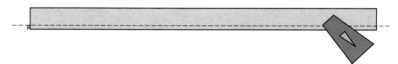

- Move the iron with an up and down motion, zigzagging along the seam rather than ironing down the length of the seam which could cause distortion.
- Open up your strips and press on the *right* side of the fabric towards the darker fabric, if necessary guiding the seam underneath to make sure the seam is going in the right direction (see diagram below). Press with an up and down motion rather than along the length of the strip.

- Always take care if using steam and certainly don't use steam anywhere near a bias edge, as this could stretch the fabric.
- When you are joining more than two strips together, press the seams after attaching each strip. You are far more likely to get bowing if you leave it until your strip unit is complete before pressing.
- Each seam must be pressed flat before another seam is sewn across it. Unless there is a special reason for not doing so, seams are pressed towards the darker fabric. The main criteria when joining seams, however, is to have the seam allowances going in the opposite direction to each other as they then nest together without bulk. Your patchwork will lie flat and your seam intersections will be accurate.

Pinning

Don't underestimate the benefits of pinning. When you have to align a seam it is important to insert pins to stop any movement when sewing. Long, fine pins with flat heads are recommended as they will go through the layers of fabric easily and allow you to sew up to and over them.

Aways press seams in opposite directions so they nest together nicely. Insert a pin either at right angles or diagonally through the seam intersection, ensuring that the seams match perfectly. When sewing, do not remove the pin too early as your fabric might shift and your seams will not be perfectly aligned.

Chain Piecing

Chain piecing is the technique of feeding a series of pieces through the sewing machine without lifting the presser foot and without cutting the thread between each piece (see diagram below). Always chain piece when you can, as it saves time and thread. Once your chain is complete simply snip the thread between the pieces.

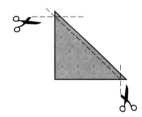

When chain piecing shapes other than squares and rectangles it is sometimes preferable when finishing one shape, to lift the presser foot slightly and reposition on the next shape, still leaving the thread uncut.

Dog Ears to Go

A dog ear is the excess piece of fabric that overlaps past the seam allowance when sewing triangles to other shapes. Dog ears should always be cut off to reduce bulk. They can be trimmed using a rotary cutter although snipping with small sharp scissors is quicker. Make sure you are trimming the points parallel to the straight edge of the triangle

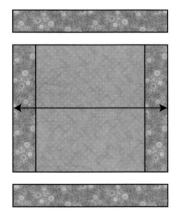

Adding borders

The fabric requirements in this book all assume you are going to be sewing straight rather than mitred borders. If you intend to have mitred borders please add sufficient fabric for this.

1. Begin by sewing all your border strips into one continuous length. These strips may be straight from the jelly roll or layer cake or cut from separate fabric, according to the instructions given for each quilt.

2. Determine the vertical measurement from top to bottom through the centre of your quilt top. Cut two side border strips to this measurement. Mark the halves and quarters of one quilt side and one border with pins. Placing right sides together and matching the pins, stitch quilt and border together, easing the quilt side to fit where necessary. Repeat on the opposite side.

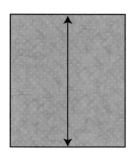

3. Now determine the horizontal measurement from side to side across the centre of the quilt top. Cut two top and bottom border strips to this measurement and add to the quilt top in the same manner as before.

Quilting

Quilting stitches hold the patchwork top, wadding and backing together and create texture over your finished patchwork. The choice is yours whether you hand quilt, machine quilt or send it off to a longarm quilting service. There are many books showing the techniques of hand and machine quilting but the basic procedure is as follows:

1. With the aid of templates or a ruler, mark out the quilting lines on the patchwork top.

2. Cut the backing and wadding at least 3in larger all around than the patchwork top. Pin or tack the layers together to prepare them for quilting.

3. Quilt either by hand or by machine.

Binding your Quilt

The fabric requirements in this book are for a 2½in double-fold French binding cut on the straight of grain.

1. Trim the excess backing and wadding so edges are even with the top of the quilt.

2. Join your binding strips into a continuous length, making sure there is sufficient to go around the quilt plus 8in–10in for the corners and overlapping ends.

3. With wrong sides together, press the binding in half lengthways. Fold and press under ½in to neaten edge at the end where you will start sewing.

4. On the right side of the quilt and starting about 12in away from one of the corners, align the edges of the double thickness binding with the edge of the quilt, so that the cut edges are towards the edges of the quilt, and pin to hold in place. Sew with a ¼in seam allowance, leaving the first inch open (see diagram, right).

Stop ¼in from the end

5. At the first corner, stop ¼in from the edge of the fabric and backstitch (see first diagram below). Lift the needle and presser foot and fold up at 45 degrees as shown, then fold down as shown in the second diagram. Stitch from the edge to ¼in from the next corner and repeat the turn.

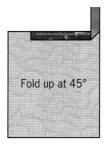

Fold up at 45°

Fold down and stitch from edge to ¼in from next corner. Repeat turn.

6. Continue around the quilt, working each corner in the same way. When you come to the starting point, cut the binding, fold under the cut edge and overlap at the starting point.

7. Fold over the binding to the back of the quilt and hand stitch in place. At each corner fold the binding to form a neat mitre.

How to Calculate Fabric for a Larger Quilt

In this book we have included two large quilts that use a combination of one jelly roll and one layer cake but the remaining quilts show what can be achieved with just one jelly roll or just one layer cake. We have sometimes added background fabric and borders but the basis of each quilt is just one – or in the case of charm packs, just a few!

If you want to make a larger version of any quilt, refer to the Vital Statistics of the quilt, which shows the block size, the number of blocks, how the blocks are set plus the border size. You can then calculate your requirements if making a larger quilt.

Tips for Setting on Point

Razzle Dazzle and Raspberry Ripple are both examples of quilts set diagonally or 'on point'. The patterns contain all the information you need to make the quilt. However, any block can take on a totally new look when set on point and you might like to try one of the other quilts to see what it looks like on point. For this reason we have included information for setting quilts on point. Some people are a little daunted as there are a few points to take into consideration but here is all you need to know.

- **How wide will my blocks be when set on point?**
To calculate the measurement of the block from point to point you multiply the size of the finished block by 1.414.
Example: a 12in block will measure 12in x 1.414 which is 16.97in – just under 17in. Now you can calculate how many blocks you need for your quilt.

- **How do I piece blocks on point?**
Piece rows diagonally, starting at a corner. Triangles have to be added to the end of each row *before* joining the rows and these are called setting triangles.

• How do I calculate what size setting triangles to cut?

Setting triangles form the outside of your quilt and need to have the straight of grain on the outside edge to prevent stretching. To ensure this, these triangles are formed from quarter-square triangles, i.e. a square cut into four. The measurement for this is: Diagonal block size + 1¼in.

Example: a 12in block (diagonal measurement approx. 17in) should be 18¼in.

Corners triangles are added last. They also need to have the outside edge on the straight of grain so these should be cut from half-square triangles. To calculate the size of the square to cut in half, divide the finished size of your block by 1.414 and add ⅞in. Example: a 12in block would be 12in divided by 1.414 = 8.49in + ⅞in (0.88in) = 9.37in (or 9½in as it can be trimmed later).

The type of diagonal quilt that we have used in this book starts off with one block and in each row thereafter the number of blocks increases by two. All rows contain an odd number of blocks. To calculate the finished size of the quilt, you count the number of diagonals across and multiply this by the diagonal measurement of the block. Do the same with the number of blocks down and multiply this by the diagonal measurement of the block.

If you want a rectangular quilt instead of a square one, you count the number of blocks in the row that establishes the width (see diagram below) and repeat that number in following rows until the desired length is established.

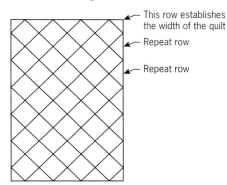

This row establishes the width of the quilt

Repeat row

Repeat row

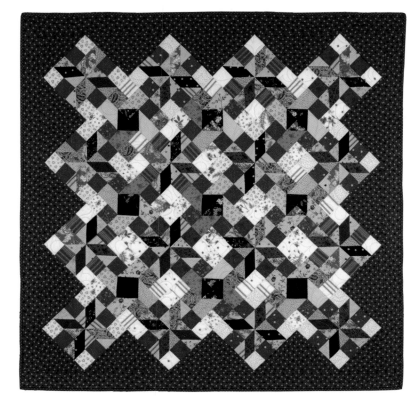

Calculating Backing Fabric Requirements

Our patterns do not include fabric requirements for backing as many people like to use wide backing fabric so they do not have to have any joins.

• Using 60in or 90in wide fabric

It is a simple calculation as to how much fabric you need to buy.

Example: your quilt is 54in x 72in. Your backing needs to be 3in larger all round so your backing measurement is 60in x 78in. If you have found 60in wide backing, then you would buy the length, which is 78in. However, if you have found 90in wide backing, you can turn it round and you would only have to buy the width of 60in.

• Using 42in wide fabric

You will need to have a join or joins in order to get the required measurement unless the backing measurement for your quilt is 42in or less on one side. If your backing measurements is less than 42in then you need only buy one length.

Using the previous example, if one of your backing measurement is 60in x 78in, you will have to have one seam somewhere in your backing. If you join two lengths of 42in fabric together your new fabric measurement will be 84in (less a little for the seam). This would be sufficient for the length of your quilt so you need to buy two times the width, i.e. 60in x 2 = 120in. Your seam will run horizontally.

If your quilt length is more than your new backing fabric measurement of 84in you will need to use the measurement of 84in for the width of your quilt and you will have to buy two times the length. Your seam will then run vertically.

Razzle Dazzle (see page 80) is an example of how striking a quilt can look when the blocks are set on point. A border made in the same fabric as the setting triangles creates a stunning, unified look to the quilt.

Useful Contacts

The Quilt Room
Shop: 20 West Street, Dorking, Surrey
RH4 1BL, UK
Tel: 01306 740739
Mail Order: 37A High Street, Dorking,
Surrey, RH4 1AR, UK
Tel: 01306 877307
www.quiltroom.co.uk

Moda Fabrics/United Notions
13800 Hutton Drive, Dallas,
Texas 75234, USA
Tel: 800-527-9447
www.modafabrics.com

Creative Grids (UK) Ltd
Unit 1J Peckleton Lane Business Park
Peckleton Lane, Peckleton, Leicester
LE9 7RN, UK
Tel: 01455 828667
www.creativegrids.com

Lecien Fabric
(European Distributor)
Rhinetex B.V., Geurdeland 7
6673 Dr. Andelst, Netherlands
Tel: 31-488-480030
www.rhinetex.com

Lecien Fabric
(US Distributor)
The Gary L. Marcus Co Inc.
11 Brownwood Lane, Norwich
CT. 06360, USA
Tel: 860-887-6614
Email: glmarcusco@aol.com
For other countries see Lecien website:
www.lecien.co.jp

Daiwabo Co Ltd
(Japanese taupes)
For shops and distributor information
visit www.pinwheelstrading.com

**Kaffe Fassett, Heather Bailey and
Tanya Whelan Fabrics**
(European Distributor)
Rowan Yarns, Green Lane Mill
Holmfirth, HD9 2DX, UK
Tel: 01484 681881

**Kaffe Fassett, Heather Bailey and
Tanya Whelan Fabrics**
(US Distributor)
Rowan Yarns, 4 Townsend West, Suite 8
Nashua, N.H. 03063, USA
Tel: (603) 886 5041

Mary Ellen Hopkins
#18 Vista Terrace, Pacific Palisades
California 90272-4655
www.maryellenhopkins.com

Thirties Fabrics by Marcus Brothers
www.marcusbrothers.com
or Anbo Textiles (European Distributor)
Unit 8–9 Dashwood Industrial Estate
Dashwood Avenue, High Wycombe
Bucks, HP12 3ED, UK

Zen Roses Fabrics
Makower UK Ltd, 118 Greys Road
Henley-on-Thames, Oxfordshire
RG9 1QW, UK
Tel: 01491 579727
www.makoweruk.com

Acknowledgments

Pam and Nicky would firstly like to thank Mark Dunn at Moda for his continued support and for allowing them to use the names of Jelly Rolls and Layer Cakes in the title and throughout the book. They hope their obvious appreciation of his fabrics in some way repays him. Thanks also go to Susan Rogers at Moda who looks after them so well and makes sure that they see all the new ranges, and thanks to the rest of the team at Moda who couldn't be more helpful.

Their thanks also go to Jane Trollope and the team at David & Charles for making their journey with jelly rolls so exciting – no one realized quite how exciting it would be!

Last but not least, special thanks to Pam's husband Nick for allowing the dust to accumulate and the weeds to take over the garden, and to Nicky's partner Rob for his encouragement for all she does and who readily takes over the chores when the sewing machine is on full throttle!

About the Authors

Pam Lintott opened her shop, The Quilt Room, in 1981, which she still runs today, along with her daughter Nicky. Pam is the author of *The Quilt Room, Patchwork & Quilting Workshops*, as well as *The Quilter's Workbook*.

Nicky has been working at The Quilt Room for a number of years and has now taken over the day-to-day running of the business, to allow her very appreciative mother more time to look after her dogs and chickens! She also runs the longarm quilting service very successfully.

Layer Cake, Jelly Roll and Charm Quilts is Pam and Nicky's second book for David & Charles, following on from their phenomenally successful *Jelly Roll Quilts*.

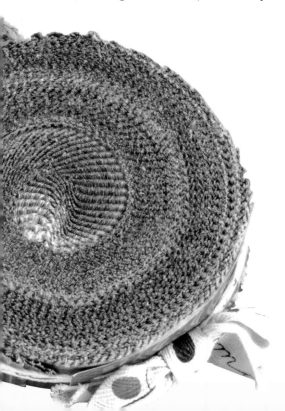

Index